30 Korean Short Stories for Complete Beginners

Grow Your Korean Vocabulary by Reading and Listening to Short Stories

©All rights reserved 2020
Frédéric BIBARD (FluentinKorean.com)

No part of this book including the audio material may be copied, reproduced, transmitted or distributed in any form without prior written permission of the author. For permission requests, write to: Frédéric BIBARD at contact@fluentinkorean.com

For more products by Frédéric BIBARD, visit

https://fluentinkorean.com/

TABLE OF CONTENTS

INTRODUCTION vii

STORY 1: FIRST DAY - PART 1 1
    DIFFICULT WORDS 3
    SUMMARY OF THE STORY: 3
    QUIZ: 4

STORY 2: FIRST DAY - PART 2 5
    DIFFICULT WORDS 7
    SUMMARY OF THE STORY: 7
    QUIZ: 8

STORY 3: FIRST DAY - PART 3 9
    DIFFICULT WORDS 11
    SUMMARY OF THE STORY: 11
    QUIZ: 12

STORY 4: GOING ON HOLIDAY – PART 1 13
    DIFFICULT WORDS 15
    SUMMARY OF THE STORY: 15
    QUIZ: 16

STORY 5: GOING ON HOLIDAY – PART 2 18
    DIFFICULT WORDS 20
    SUMMARY OF THE STORY: 20
    QUIZ: 21

STORY 6: FOOD SHOPPING ABROAD 22
    DIFFICULT WORDS 24
    SUMMARY OF THE STORY: 24
    QUIZ: 25

STORY 7: A BUSY DAY IN THE HOLIDAYS (1) 26
    DIFFICULT WORDS 29
    SUMMARY OF THE STORY: 29
    QUIZ: 30

STORY 8: CHOCOLATE CAKE 31
    DIFFICULT WORDS 33
    SUMMARY OF THE STORY: 33
    QUIZ: 34

STORY 9: HOW TO BAKE SCONES..35
DIFFICULT WORDS..37
SUMMARY OF THE STORY:..37
QUIZ:...38

STORY 10: INTERNET..39
DIFFICULT WORDS..41
SUMMARY OF THE STORY:..41
QUIZ:...42

STORY 11: CHANNEL TUNNEL..44
DIFFICULT WORDS..47
SUMMARY OF THE STORY:..47
QUIZ:...48

STORY 12: WEATHER REPORT..49
DIFFICULT WORDS..51
SUMMARY OF THE STORY:..51
QUIZ:...52

STORY 13: A BUSY DAY IN THE HOLIDAYS (2).................................53
DIFFICULT WORDS..55
SUMMARY OF THE STORY:..55
QUIZ:...56

STORY 14: SMARTPHONES..57
DIFFICULT WORDS..59
QUIZ:...60

STORY 15: CHESTER...61
DIFFICULT WORDS..63
SUMMARY OF THE STORY:..63
QUIZ:...64

STORY 16: A FAMILY HOLIDAY – PART 1..65
DIFFICULT WORDS..67
SUMMARY OF THE STORY:..67
QUIZ:...68

STORY 17: A FAMILY HOLIDAY – PART 2..69
DIFFICULT WORDS..71
SUMMARY OF THE STORY :...71
QUIZ:...72

STORY 18: A FAMILY HOLIDAY – PART 3 .... **73**
   DIFFICULT WORDS 75
   SUMMARY OF THE STORY : 75
   QUIZ: 76

STORY 19: A FAMILY HOLIDAY – PART 4 .... **77**
   DIFFICULT WORDS 79
   SUMMARY OF THE STORY : 79
   QUIZ: 80

STORY 20: A FAMILY HOLIDAY – PART 5 .... **81**
   DIFFICULT WORDS 83
   SUMMARY OF THE STORY : 83
   QUIZ: 84

STORY 21: GETTING HOME **85**
   DIFFICULT WORDS 88
   SUMMARY OF THE STORY : 88
   QUIZ: 89

STORY 22: OUT SHOPPING AND FOR LUNCH (1) **90**
   DIFFICULT WORDS 92
   SUMMARY OF THE STORY : 92
   QUIZ: 93

STORY 23: OUT SHOPPING AND FOR LUNCH (2) **94**
   DIFFICULT WORDS 96
   SUMMARY OF THE STORY : 96
   QUIZ: 97

STORY 24: OUT SHOPPING AND FOR LUNCH (3) **98**
   DIFFICULT WORDS 100
   SUMMARY OF THE STORY : 100
   QUIZ: 101

STORY 25: END OF THE HOLIDAYS (1) **102**
   DIFFICULT WORDS 104
   SUMMARY OF THE STORY : 104
   QUIZ: 105

STORY 26: END OF THE HOLIDAYS (2) **106**
   DIFICULLT WORDS 110
   SUMMARY OF THE STORY : 110
   QUIZ: 111

STORY 27: END OF THE HOLIDAYS (3)..112
DIFFICULT WORDS 114
SUMMARY OF THE STORY :...114
QUIZ:..115

STORY 28: END OF THE HOLIDAYS (4)..116
DIFFICULT WORDS 118
SUMMARY OF THE STORY :...118
QUIZ:..119

STORY 29: END OF THE HOLIDAYS (5)..120
DIFFICULT WORDS 122
SUMMARY OF THE STORY :...122
QUIZ:..123

STORY 30: END OF THE HOLIDAYS (6)..124
DIFFICULT WORDS 126
SUMMARY OF THE STORY :...126
QUIZ:..127

CONCLUSION 128

HOW TO DOWNLOAD THE AUDIO? 129

ABOUT FLUENT IN KOREAN..130

INTRODUCTION

Everybody loves stories. I'm sure you do, too. So how would you like to learn Korean with the help of very short stories? It's fun and easy!

Most students who learn Korean as a second language say they are having the most trouble with the following issues:

- Lack of vocabulary
- Difficulty in picking up grammar structures, and
- Hesitation in speaking Korean because of (1) pronunciation troubles or (2) listening comprehension problems.

This collection of 30 very short stories will help you solve those challenges. At only 300 words per story, this book is created for complete beginners with little to no previous experience in learning Korean.

Learn new vocabulary

The stories in this book are written using the most useful Korean words. After each story, you will find a list of vocabulary used in the story together with its Korean translation. There is no need to reach for a dictionary each time you encounter words you don't understand, and you will quickly learn new words as you go along.

Easily grasp Korean sentence structures

Written with a good mix of descriptive sentences and simple dialogue, the stories will introduce you to different types of sentence structures. This way, you'll be able to naturally pick up Korean grammar structures as you read the stories.

Practice your listening comprehension

To be able to speak Korean well, you need to expose your ears to a lot of spoken Korean. You can do that by listening to the free audio narration of the stories. Listen to the words out loud and compare them to the written stories. Read along to the narration. Copy the correct pronunciation and practice the inflections. With enough practice, you will soon be able to get over your hesitations in speaking Korean.

Learning Korean as a second language can be a scary task. But with these short stories, you can make it as fun and as easy as possible. Before you know it, you have already learned hundreds of new Korean words, exposed yourself to a variety of sentence structures, and listened to enough spoken Korean that your pronunciation will improve greatly.

So go ahead. Start reading and have some fun!

Best of luck!

Fluent in Korean Team

이야기 1: 첫째 날 - 파트 1
STORY 1: FIRST DAY - PART 1

IMPORTANT: Please check at the end of the book how you can download the audio.

알람은 7시에 맞춰져 있지만, 나는 일찍 일어났다. 지금은 6시 30분. 나는 설레면서도 초조한 기분이다.

The alarm is set for 07:00 but I wake up early. It is 6:30. I am excited and nervous at the same time.

오늘은 월요일이고 내가 새 직장에 출근하는 날이다.

It's Monday and today is the day I start my new job.

나는 일어나 샤워를 한다. 그리고 아침을 먹는다. 배가 고프지는 않지만, 약간의 커피와 바나나를 먹는다. 점심으로 먹을 샌드위치를 만든다.

I get up and take a shower. Then I have breakfast. I am not hungry but drink some coffee and eat a banana. I make myself a sandwich for my lunch.

나는 옷을 입으러 간다. 정장과 블라우스를 고른다. 거울을 본다. 내 생각에 너무 격식 있는 것 같아서 생각을 바꾼다. 어두운색의 원피스와 어울리는 재킷을 찾아 훨씬 편안한 느낌이다.

I go to get dressed. I choose a smart suit and blouse. I look in the mirror. I think I look too formal and change my mind. I find a dark coloured dress and matching jacket and feel much more comfortable.

이를 닦고 화장을 한다.

I clean my teeth and put on some make-up.

차 열쇠를 찾은 후 시간을 확인하고 나서야 출근하기에 조금 이르다는 것을 알았다. 지금은 7시 15분인데 나는 8시 30분까지 출근이다!

I find my car keys and then check the time, and realise that I am very early. It is 7:15 and I start work at 08:30!

어쨌든 이 시간 교통 상황을 잘 모르니 빨리 나가기로 한다. 나는 피터와 헨리에게 다녀온다고 인사한다.

I decide to leave anyway as I don't know what the traffic is like at this time. I say goodbye to Peter and Henry.

나는 8시쯤 늦지 않게 도착해서, 주차장에 차를 주차하고, 나의 새로운 사무실 문으로 향한다. 가는 데까지 3분이 걸린다.

I arrive in good time, at about 08:00, park my car in the car park, and make my way to the door of my new office. It takes me 3 minutes to walk there.

문을 두드린다. 내 상사인 쟈넷이 문으로 나와 들여보내 준다.

I knock on the door. My boss, Janet, comes to the door and lets me in.

어떤 사람들은 벌써 일하고 있고 그녀는 나를 새 동료들에게 소개한다. 그녀는, "새 사무실 매니저인 사라씨입니다." 라고 말한다.

Some people are already working and she introduces me to my new colleagues. She says, "This is Sarah. She's the new office manager".

모두가 매우 다정하게 내가 소개하자 "반가워요", "안녕하세요", "만나서 반갑습니다" 라고 말한다.

Everybody is very friendly and they say "Hello", "Hi" and "Pleased to meet you," as I am introduced to them.

쟈넷은 나에게 화장실과 주방은 어디에 있는지 보여주고, 내 책상을 보여준다. 나는 일을 시작하기 위해 자리에 앉는다.

Janet shows me where the toilets are, and the kitchen, then she shows me to my desk. I sit down to start work.

배울 것이 많아 아침이 아주 금방 지나간다.

I have a lot to learn and the morning passes very quickly.

얼마 지나지 않아, 점심시간이다. 나는 주방으로 가서 내 샌드위치를 먹고 커피를 만들기로 한다.

Before long, it is lunchtime. I decide to go to the kitchen to eat my sandwich and make some coffee.

가방을 열고 안을 들여다본다.

I open my bag and I look inside.

가방을 비운다. 내가 꺼낸 모든 물건을 본다. 샌드위치가 어디에 있지?

I empty out my bag. I look at everything I have taken out. Where is the sandwich?

다시 본다. 여전히 샌드위치는 없다.

I look again. Still there is no sandwich.

그냥 커피로 점심을 때우기로 한다.

Just coffee for lunch then.

Difficult Words

1- 옷을 입다 – To get dressed
2- 정장 – A smart suit
3- 블라우스 – A blouse
4- 아침(식사) – Breakfast
5- 화장을 하다 – Put on make-up
6- 교통(량) – Traffic/ circulation
7- 상사 – Boss
8- 사무실 니저 – Office manager
9- 부엌 – The kitchen
10- 나는 앉는다 – I sit down
11- 점심(식사) – Lunch
12- J'ai emport (inf : emporter) – I took
13- 만나서 반갑습니다 – Nice to meet you
14- 일하다 – To work
15- 어울리는 재킷 – A matching jacket

이야기 요약 :

흥분되기도 하고 초조하기도 한 한편, 사라는 오늘 새로운 일을 시작할 준비가 되어 있다. 그녀는 첫날을 잘 준비하기 위해 시간을 쏟고 회사에도 일찍 도착하지만 무언가 계획대로 되지 않는 일이 생긴다.

Summary of the Story:

Feeling excited and nervous, Sarah is ready to start her new job today. She takes time to prepare well for her first day and arrives early, but something is not going as planned.

Quiz:

1) 사라가 점심으로 먹은것은 무엇인가요?
   a) 샌드위치와 커피
   b) 바나나와 커피
   c) 커피만

1) What does Sarah eat for lunch?
   a) A sandwich and a coffee
   b) A banana and a coffee
   c) Only a coffee

2) 사라는 :
   a) 새로운 오피스 매니저
   b) 쟈넷의 후임자
   c) 새로운 상사

2) Sarah is:
   a) The new office manager
   b) Janette's new replacement
   c) The new boss

3) 쟈넷은 :
   a) 사라의 동료
   b) 사라의 친구
   c) 사라의 상사

3) Janette is:
   a) The colleague of Sarah.
   b) The friend of Sarah.
   c) The boss of Sarah.

ANSWERS:
   1) C
   2) A
   3) C

이야기 2: 첫째 날 - 파트 2
STORY 2: FIRST DAY - PART 2

나는 커피를 가지고 직원 주방에 앉아 휴대전화 메시지를 본다. 많은 친구가 새로 시작하는 직장의 첫날에 " 행운을 빌어 " 라고 메시지를 보내온다.

I sit with my coffee in the staff kitchen and look at my phone messages. Lots of friends are sending me "good luck" messages for my first day in my new job.

동료들이 한둘씩 주방으로 들어오기 시작하는데 모두 친근하게 안녕하세요하고 인사한다. 모두 내가 앉아 있는 곳에 점심을 가지고 같이 앉는다.

My colleagues start to come into the kitchen in ones and twos and they are all friendly and say hello. They come over to where I am sitting and join me with their lunch.

그들은 나에 대해, 내가 어디에 사는지, 사귀는 사람은 있는지, 이전에 어떤 일을 했는지 같은 것을 묻는다.

They ask me questions about myself, where I live, if I'm in a relationship, what other jobs I have done, and so on.

그러면, 이렇게 대답한다:

So, here are the answers:

내 이름은 사라이고 38살이다.

My name is Sarah and I am 38 years old.

나는 슬림 브릿지라는 사무실에서 25㎞ 떨어진 작은마을에 살고 있다. 거기에는 150 여 개의 집과 술집, 우체국, 신문 가게, 식료품점이 있다. 마을 중앙에는 교회가 있고 아이들이 자주 찾는 축구 경기장과 테니스코트가 있는 공원이 있다.

I live in Slimbridge which is a small village about 25 kms away from the office. There are about 150 houses there, a pub, a post office and newsagent, and a grocery store. The church is at the centre of the village and there is a park with football pitches and tennis courts where all the children go to play.

나는 선생님인 피터와 결혼한 지 11년째이고 8살인 아들 헨리가 있다. 헨리는 활력이 넘치고 항상 분주하다. 우리는 스포츠를 즐기며 헨리는 마을 축구팀에 속해있다. 그는 매주 토요일 아침마다 경기하며 피터와 나는 함께 도우러 가려고 노력한다.

I have been married to Peter, a teacher, for 11 years and we have a son, Henry, who is 8 years old. Henry is full of energy and wants to be busy. We all like to do sport and Henry is in the village football team. He plays matches on a Saturday morning, and Peter and I go along to help when we can.

남편과 나는 겨울에는 배드민턴을 즐기고 여름에는 테니스를 즐긴다. 우리는 헨리와 함께 수영도 자주 가려고 노력한다.

My husband and I play badminton in the winter months and tennis during the summer. We go swimming with Henry as often as we can.

내가 맡은 일은 모두 관리가 포함되어 있고 사무실에서 하는 일이다. 나는 서류 작업에 능숙하고 정리정돈도 잘한다. 나는 5년 동안 은행에서 일했고 부서를 관리했으며 헨리가 태어났을 때 그만두었다.

All of my jobs have involved administration and working in an office. I am good at paperwork and am very organised. I worked for a bank for five years, managing a department, and left there when Henry was born.

이제 그들은 나를 더 잘 이해한다.

So now they know me better.

점심시간이 끝나고 우리는 이야기를 나누고 미소를 지으며 사무실로 돌아간다.

The lunch break ends and we all go back to the office chatting and smiling.

Difficult Words

1- 메세지를 보낸다 – Sending me
2- 나와 함께하다 – Join me
3- 행운을 빌다 – Good luck
4- ~에 살다 – I live
5- 일/ 직업 – Jobs
6- 내 이름은 – My name is
7- 식료품점 – Grocery store
8- 교회 – Church
9- (게임/스포츠 경기를) 하다 – To play
10- 선생님 – Teacher
11- 아들 – Son
12- 겨울 – Winter
13- 여름 – Summer
14- 사무실 – Office
15- 서류 작업 – Paperwork

이야기 요약 :

사라는 계속해서 그녀의 첫날을 보내고 동료들과 사교활동을 하는데, 그들은 그녀에 대해 많은 질문들을 한다

Summary of the Story:

Sarah continues her first day at work and socializes with her colleagues who ask her a lot of questions about her.

Quiz:

1) 사라가 사는 마을에 없는 것은 :

   a) 술집

   b) 식료품점

   c) 병원

1) In the village where Sarah lives, there is not:

   a) A bar

   b) A grocerie store

   c) A hospital

2) 사라와 피터가 결혼한 기간은 얼마인가요?

   a) 8 년

   b) 11 년

   c) 25 년

2) Sarah and Peter have been married for how many years?

   a) 8 years

   b) 11 years

   c) 25 years

3) 사라네 부부가 여름 동안 즐기는 스포츠는 :

   a) 배드민턴

   b) 축구

   c) 테니스

3) During the summer, Sarah and her husband play:

   a) Badminton

   b) Football

   c) Tennis

ANSWERS:

   1) C

   2) B

   3) C

이야기 3 : 첫째 날 - 파트 3
STORY 3: FIRST DAY - PART 3

근무시간이 끝나고 나는 집에 돌아갈 길을 생각한다. 지금은 5시 30분이다.

The working day comes to an end and I think about my journey home. It is 17:30.

나는 모두가 떠날 때까지 기다렸다가 가방을 들고 사무실 열쇠를 가지고 나간다. 이제 내가 사무실 매니저라서, 매일 아침 사무실을 열고 잠그는 것은 내 책임이다. 그래서, 내가 아침 제일 먼저 출근해야 한다.

I wait for everybody to leave then pick up my bag and take out the office keys. I am responsible for locking the office, and opening it each morning, now that I am the office manager. So, I need to arrive first in the morning.

보안 알람 설정과 창문 확인도 해야 한다. 또한, 컴퓨터가 꺼졌는지도 확인해야만 한다. 내가 이 모든 것을 다 하는데 15분 정도 걸린다. 내일은 더 빨리할 수 있으리라 생각한다.

There is a security alarm to set as well as windows to check. And I must make sure the computers have been switched off. I do all of that and it takes me about 15 minutes. I'm sure I will be quicker tomorrow.

나는 운전해 나가 교통체증을 겪는다. 25km 거리의 집까지 한 시간이 좀 넘게 걸린다. 집에 6시 45분에 도착한다.

I drive away in my car and join a traffic jam. It takes me more than an hour to drive the 25 kms home. I get home at 18:45.

느리게 운전하는 동안 차 대신 기차나 버스 통근을 고려한다.

I spend the slow driving thinking about travelling by train or by bus instead of by car.

다음은 내 선택 가능성이다:

These are my options:

- 버스 정류장은 집에서 걸어서 단지 5분 거리이며 버스는 1시간 간격으로 15분마다 도착한다. 여정은 한 시간 정도 걸린다. 버스 정류장에 내리면, 걸어서 15분 정도 걸린다. 7시 15분에 버스를 타려면, 집에서 7시 10분에 나가야 하고, 오늘 아침보다 5분 일찍 나와야 한다. 내 생각에 사무실에는 8시 30분까지 도착할 것 같다. 8시 30분에 일을 시작하기 때문에 조금 빠듯하다.

- The bus stop is only 5 minutes' walk from my house and the buses run once per hour at a quarter past. The journey takes a full hour. When I get off at the bus station, I have a 15-minute walk ahead of me. If I take the bus at 0715, I will leave the house by 0710, 5 minutes earlier than this morning. I think I will arrive at the office at 0830. That's tight as I start work at 0830.
- 기차역은 집에서 운전으로 10분 거리에 있으며 거기에는 작은 주차장이 있다. 기차는 매 30분 간격인 5분과 35분마다 있다. 여정은 25분 걸린다. 기차역에서 사무실까지는 걸어서 10분 걸린다. 기차를 타기 위해서, 7시 15분에는 집을 나서야 - 차를 주차하고 정류장까지 가기 위해 - 7시 35분 기차를 탈 수 있다. 8시에 기차에서 내려 사무실에는 8시 10분까지 갈 수 있다.
- The train station is a 10-minute drive from home and there is little parking there. The trains run every half hour at 5 and 35 minutes past each hour. The journey takes 25 minutes. The walk from the station to my office is 10 minutes. To take the train, I need to leave home at 07:15 – to be sure to be able to park, and to get to the platform – for the train at 07:35. I get off the train at 08:00 and can be at the office for 08:10.

집에 도착해서, 버스와 기차로 통근할 때의 요금을 확인한다. 나는 운전하는 것과 비용을 비교해 본다 - 주차 비용과 휘발유 가격까지.

When I get home, I check the cost of travelling by bus and travelling by train. I compare the costs with travelling by car - paying for the car park as well as the cost of the petrol.

비용에 상관없이, 나는 편리함이 더 중요하다고 생각해 계속 운전하기로 한다.

Regardless of the cost, I decide that convenience is more important and I will continue to travel by car.

Difficult Words

1- 집 – House
2- 나는 기다린다 – I wait
3- 나는 들다 – I take/ I pick up
4- 열쇄 – Keys
5- 먼저, 첫번째로 – First
6- 닫기/ 잠그기 – Closing/ locking
7- 창문 – Windows
8- 나는 확인한다 – I check
9- 컴퓨터들 – Computers
10- 끄다 – Switched off
11- 교통 체증 – Traffic jam
12- 통근, 출퇴근 – A travel
13- 주차 – Parking
14- 주차하다 – To park
15- 비용 – Costs

이야기 요약 :

사라가 첫날 일을 마치고 집으로 돌아간다. 교통 체증으로 인해 가는 길은 느렸고 그녀는 통근을 위한 다른 방안들을 생각해 보기 시작한다.

Summary of the Story:

Sarah ends her first day at work and returns home. Along the way, she is slowed down by traffic and starts considering her other options for getting to work.

Quiz:

1) 왜 사라는 계속 자가용으로 통근하기로 결정 하였나요?
   a) 자가용 출근이 기차보다 비용이 적게 들어서
   b) 자가용이 보다 편리해서
   c) 자가용 이용이 시간이 적게 걸려서

1) Why did Sarah choose to continue to drive her car to work?
   a) Because the car is cheaper than the train.
   b) Because the car is more convenient.
   c) Because she can save time by taking the car

2) 사라가 집에 도착하기까지 얼마나 걸렸나요?
   a) 한 시간 이상
   b) 23분
   c) 45락

2) How long does it take for Sarah to arrive home?
   a) More than an hour
   b) 25 minutes
   c) 45 minutes

3) 사라가 기차를 이용한다면 몇 시에 사무실에 도착하나요?
   a) 8시
   b) 7시 35분
   c) 8시10분

3) What time would Sarah arrive at the office if she'll take the train?
   a) 8h
   b) 7h35
   c) 8h10

ANSWERS:
   1) B
   2) A
   3) C

이야기 4: 휴가 보내기 - 파트 1
STORY 4: GOING ON HOLIDAY – PART 1

휴가를 계획할 때는 생각할 것이 많다.

There is a lot to think about when you are planning a holiday.

첫 번째로, 어디에 갈지 결정해야 한다. 가고 싶은 목적지가 있는가? 있을 수도 있지만, 없을 수도 있다.

Firstly, you need to decide where to go. Do you have a destination in mind? You may have, but you may not.

활동적인 휴가를 가고 싶을 수도 있고, 아마 다른 문화나 언어를 배울 수 있는 휴가를 원하거나, 휴가 기간 내내 수영장이나 해변에 누워 아무것도 하지 않고 쉬고 싶을 수도 있다. 아니면 이 세 가지 모두를 원할 수도 있고.

You may want to go on an activity holiday, or perhaps a holiday to learn about a different culture or language, or you may want to lie by a pool or on a beach and do nothing but relax for the duration of your holiday. Or perhaps a combination of all 3.

어떻게 시간을 보내고 싶은지를 결정해야만 한다.

You have to decide on how you want to spend your time.

그리고 누구와 함께 갈지도 결정해야 하는데, 특히 당신과 당신의 일행이 어디에 갈지, 무엇을 할지 의견을 맞출 수 없다면 말이다.

And you may also have to decide who to go with, especially if you and your travel party can't agree on where you're going or what you're doing.

현실적으로, 선택할 곳은 한계가 없고 그 말은 결정하기도 힘들다는 뜻이다. 인터넷은 어마어마한 종류의 아이디어와 목적지, 취미를 생각해 볼 수 있게 해 주고, 이제까지 가능했던 어느 때보다 훨씬 진취적으로 만들어 준다.

In reality, your options are almost endless, but so are the decisions to be made. The Internet enables you to consider a vast range of ideas, destinations and activities, and to be more adventurous than it has ever been possible to be.

따라 할 수 있는 단계들이 여기에 있다:

So here are the steps to take:

1) 누구와 함께 갈지 결정하라.

1) Decide who you are going to go away with.

2) 예산을 정하라.

2) Agree your budget.

3) 둘 다(또는 모두) 떠날 수 있는 날짜를 결정하라.

3) Agree dates when you are both (or all) able to get away.

4) 어떻게 시간을 보낼 것인지 의논하라 – 분주하게 보낼지, 활동적으로 보낼지, 문화적으로 보낼지, 한가하게 보낼지 아니면 모두 함께 다른 것을 할지. 그것도 아니면 이 모든 것을 조합해서 할지. 만약 모든 것을 다 같이할 수 없다면 일정 중 '각자 하고 싶은 것 하기' 시간을 가지는데 동의할 수도 있겠다.

4) Discuss how you want to spend your time away – being busy, being active, being cultured, being lazy, or being something else altogether. Or a combination of them all. If you can't agree on everything, perhaps agree to 'do your own thing' for some of the time.

5) 어디에서 지내고 싶은지 이야기해 볼 시간을 가져라: 캠핑? 호텔 아니면 빌라에서? 가족과 함께? 별빛 아래에서?

5) Spend a little time talking about where you want to stay: camping? In a hotel or villa? With a family? Under the stars?

6) 휴가 전체를 같이 계획하고 싶은지, 아니면 여행사의 도움을 받을지도 고려하라.

6) Consider if you want to plan the entire holiday yourselves, or whether you welcome the help of a travel agent.

7) 나라가 정해지면, 하나의 목적지나 여러 목적지로 좁힌 후, 핵심 활동을 정하라.

7) Agree your country, then narrow it down to your actual destination or destinations, and the key activities.

이 정도까지 왔으면, 이제 우리가 어떻게 실제로 이 계획을 실천할 수 있는지 생각해보자.

Now that you've got this far, let's think about how we actually make this happen.

Difficult Words

1- 휴가 – Holiday
2- 배우다 – To learn
3- 누워있다, 눕다 – To lie
4- 수영장 – Pool
5- 해변 – Beach
6- 휴식 – Relax
7- 당신은 원하다 – You want
8- 가다 – To go
9- 끝없는 – Endless
10- 모험 – Adventurous
11- 게으른 – Lazy
12- 별 – Stars
13- 도움 – Help
14- 나라 – Country
15- 생각해 봅시다 – Let's think

이야기 요약 :

휴가를 가기 위해서는 많은 준비를 해야 하는데, 이보다 더 중요한 것은, 많은 결정이 필요하다는 것이다. 누구와 함께 갈 것인가? 휴가 기간에 어떤 활동을 하고 싶은가? 예산은 어떻게 되는가? 이번 이야기는 휴가를 준비하는데 어떤 단계들이 필요한지를 설명한다.

Summary of the Story:

Going on vacation requires a lot of preparation, but more importantly, it requires to take a lot of important decisions. Who to go with? What kind of activity do you want to do during your vacation? What is your budget? This story describes the steps on what to take when preparing a vacation.

Quiz:

1) 다음 선택 중, 휴가 계획을 할 때 인터넷을 사용하는 장점이 아닌 것은 무엇인가요?

   a) 넓은 분야로의 아이디어, 목적지, 활동을 고려해 볼 수 있게 한다.

   b) 불가능을 가능하게 만든다.

   c) 지금까지보다 더 모험적이게 만든다.

1) Which of the following options is not an advantage of using the internet to plan your vacations?

   a) It enables you to consider a vast range of ideas, destinations and activities.

   b) It allows you to make the impossible possible.

   c) It enables you to be more adventurous than it has ever been possible to be.

2) 만약 당신과 당신의 동반자가 휴가 기간에 할 활동에 대해 합의를 내릴 수 없다면 다음과 같은 방법이 최선이다 :

   a) 타협을 한다; 내가 하기 싫어도 동반자가 원하는 것을 한다.

   b) 파트너를 바꾸고, 정확히 내가 하고자 하는 것을 원하는 친구를 찾는다.

   c) 잠시 동안은 각자의 것을 하는 것으로 정한다.

2) If you and your companion are unable to agree on the activities to do during your vacations, it is best to:

   a) Make compromises; do activities that your companion wants to do even if you don't want to.

   b) Change partners and find a friend who wants to do exactly what you want to do.

   c) Agree to do your own stuff for a while.

3) 휴가를 계획 할 때 마지막으로 실행해야 할 것은 무엇인가요?

   a) 예산을 정한다.

   b) 휴가 계획 전체를 스스로 정할 것인지, 여행사의 도움을 받을 것인지 고려한다.

   c) 국가를 정한다음, 실제 목적지나 목적지들을 정하고, 주요 활동을 결정한다.

3) What is the last step in taking action when planning a trip?

   a) Agree your budget.

   b) Consider if you want to plan the entire holiday yourselves, or whether you welcome the help of a travel agent.

   c) Agree your country, then narrow it down to your actual destination or destinations, and the key activities.

ANSWERS:

   1) B

   2) C

   3) C

이야기 5: 휴가 보내기 - 파트 2
STORY 5: GOING ON HOLIDAY – PART 2

우리는 휴가를 떠날 때 생각해야 할 것들이 많다는 것을 알고 있다. 스트레스가 많을 수도 있지만, 잘 정리한다면 괜찮을 것이다.

We know there is a lot to think about when you're going on holiday. It can be stressful, but it isn't if you're well-organised.

이제, 당신은 누구와 떠날지, 언제 갈지 알고 있다. 얼마를 쓸 것인지 아니면 쓸 수 있는지 알고 있고, 어디에서 지내고 싶은지, 떠나 있는 동안 무엇을 하고 싶은지 알고 있다. 무엇보다 가장 중요한 결정인, 목적지가 어디인지 알고 있다.

By now, you know who you're going with, and when. You know how much you want to spend or are able to spend, where you want to stay and what you want to do while you're away. You also know your destination, which is arguably the most important decision to be made.

여행사의 도움 없이, 혼자 계획을 하고 예약을 한다고 가정해 보자. 이 경우 비용이 좀 더 저렴하겠지만, 위험부담은 종종 더 높으므로 결코 쉬운 결정은 아니다.

Let's assume that you're arranging and booking this yourself, without the help of a travel agent. You will find the costs are lower this way, but the risks are sometimes higher, so it isn't be an easy decision.

다음의 조언과 단계들이 좀 더 쉬운 결정을 할 수 있도록 도와줄 것이다:

The following advice and steps will make things easier:

1) **믿을 수 있는 좋은 항공사를 골라라. 여행하고 싶은 날짜의 항공편이 가능한지 확인해라.**

1) Choose a good airline that you have confidence in. Check availability of flights for the dates you want to travel.

2) **지낼 장소를 찾아라. 떠나고 싶은 날짜에 숙소가 예약 가능한지 확인해라. 비용에 무엇이 포함되어 있고 무엇을 추가로 내야 하는지 생각해라.**

2) Look up places to stay. Check availability of accommodation for the dates you want to be away. Think about what is included and what is extra.

3) **떠나 있는 동안 하고 싶은 활동을 확인해라.**

3) Check out which activities match those you want to do while you are away.

4) 만약 모든 것이 맞으면, 날짜를 다시 확인하고, 항공편을 예약해라. 지내고 싶은 장소는 여러 군데일 수 있지만 맞는 항공편은 하나밖에 없을 것이므로, 항공편을 먼저 예약해라.

4) If everything matches up, check your dates again, then book your flights. You probably have more than one place to stay but there is probably only one flight that suits you, so book your flights first.

5) 날짜를 다시 한번 더 확인하고, 숙소를 예약해라.

5) Then check your dates again, and book your accommodation.

6) 이제 액티비티 예약을 계획해라. 하기 전에, 어떤 것이 가장 중요한지 결정해라. 각 액티비티를 제공하는 곳의 보험을 확인하고 안전을 중요하게 생각하는 곳인지 확인해라.

6) And now plan to book your activities. Before you do, decide which are the most important to you. Look at the insurance each activity provider offers and make sure they take your safety seriously.

7) 이제, 날짜를 한 번 더 확인하고, 액티비티를 예약해라.

7) Now, check your dates again, then go ahead and book your activities.

8) 마지막으로, 여행 보험을 즉시 챙겨라. 항공편과 숙소, 의료비용, 소지품 모두가 보험대상인지 확인해라. 얼마나 쓰는지, 모든 것이 보험 대상인지 고려해라.

8) And finally, take out travel insurance straightaway. Make sure it covers you for your flights, accommodation, medical needs, and all your belongings. Think about how much you are spending and make sure everything is covered.

이 모든 것과 함께, 안전한 장소에 영수증을 보관해라.

With everything, keep your receipts in a safe place.

이제, 앞으로는 언제든지 여행을 즐길 계획만 하면 된다.

And now, just plan to enjoy your trip, whenever it comes around.

Difficult Words

1- 스트레스가 많은 – Stressful
2- 정돈된, 잘 짜여진 – Organized
3- (돈, 비용을) 쓰다 – To spend
4- 지금, 현재 – Now
5- 이 방식으로, 이런 식으로 – This way
6- 쉬운 – Easy
7- 항공사 – Airline
8- 비행편 – Flights
9- 숙박, 숙소 – Accomodation
10- 필요 – Needs
11- 영수증 – Receipts
12- 안전한 곳 – Safe place
13- 즐기다 – Enjoy
14- 제공자, 운영자 – Provider
15- 찾아보다 – Look up

이야기 요약 :

목적지를 어디로 할지, 누구와 함께 떠날지, 숙박은 어떻게 할지, 예산은 얼마나 할지 등과 같은 중요한 결정들을 내린 후엔, 여행사의 도움 없이 계획을 세워야 할 때 따라야 할 몇몇 조언과 단계들이 있다.

Summary of the Story:

After having decided on the most important decisions to prepare your trip such as the destination, the person with whom to go with, the type of accommodation where you want to stay and the budget you have, it is important to follow several advice and steps to organize your trip without the help of a travel agent.

Quiz:

1) 활동들을 예약하기 전에 취해야 할 중요한 단계는 무엇인가요 ?
   a) 각 활동 운영자가 제공하는 보험 살펴보기
   b) 가장 저렴한 활동 선택하기
   c) 가장 덜 위험한 활동 선택하기

1) What is the important step to take before booking the activities?
   a) Look at the insurance each activity provider offers.
   b) Choose the cheapest activity.
   c) Choose the least dangerous activity.

2) 여행 보험에 반드시 포함 되어야 할 것은:
   a) 비행편만 포함되는지 확인
   b) 의료 비용
   c) 총 여행 경비

2) Travel insurance must cover:
   a) Flights only
   b) Medical needs
   c) The total amount of your spending

3) 모든 준비가 완료 된 후 해야 할 가장 중요한 것은 무엇인가요?
   a) 편하게 여행날이 다가오기를 기다린다.
   b) 영수증들을 안전하게 보관해 둔다.
   c) 비행기가 취소되는 것을 대비하여 차선책을 세운다.

3) Once all the preparation steps have been completed, what is important to do?
   a) Relax and wait for the journey to begin.
   b) Keep your receipts in a safe place.
   c) Prepare a plan B trip in case your flights are canceled.

ANSWERS:
   1) A
   2) B
   3) B

이야기 6: 해외에서의 식료품 구매
STORY 6: FOOD SHOPPING ABROAD

외국에서 식료품을 구매하는 것은 재밌으면서도 배움의 경험이 된다. 많은 문화의 다양성을 이해하게 해주며 삶의 다른 방식들에 대해서도 이해할 수 있게 된다.

Shopping for food in a foreign country is a pleasure and a learning experience. It enables you to see and understand so many cultural differences and, perhaps, to understand the different way of life.

추운 나라에서는, 그곳에 사는 사람들이 체온을 유지하기 위해 추가적인 열량이 필요하므로 음식이 대부분 기름지고 탄수화물 함량이 높다. 그들은 배를 채우고 속부터 온기를 줄 수 있는 음식을 고르는데, 이는 보통 요리가 오래 걸리는 경우가 많다. 그들은 음식을 완전히 익히기 위해, 필요하다면 몇 시간 동안 오븐을 켜 놓거나 모닥불을 올리는 것도 마다하지 않는다. 이는 추운 날씨에 추가적인 난방 수단이 되어준다. 가끔, 슈퍼마켓들은 보기에 조금 심심한 음식만 진열하는 때도 있다. 이들은 땅속이나 어둠 속에서 자라면서 빛을 충분히 보지 않아 색이 거의 없다. 결과적으로 맛이 없어 보이거나 흥미롭지 않아 보일 수 있다. 보기에는 별로 먹고 싶지 않아 보일 수 있을지 모르나, 여전히 맛있을 것이다.

In cold countries, food is often heavy and full of carbohydrates, as the people who live there need to burn extra calories to keep themselves warm. They choose foods that will fill their stomachs and warm them from the inside, and which may take a long time to cook. They are happy to have an oven on, or a fire burning, for hours if necessary, to cook their food thoroughly. It is an additional source of heat in a cold climate. Often, the supermarkets only contain food which looks a little boring. It has little colour as it's grown underground or in the dark, and sees little sun. It can therefore seem unappetising or uninteresting. It certainly looks less tempting to eat, but will still be tasty.

따뜻한 나라에서는, 반면, 사람들은 보통 요리하는 것을 선호하지 않는 편이다. 그들은 집을 더 덥게 만들 오븐이나 불에서 나오는 온기를 원하지 않을뿐더러, 뜨거운 음식을 몸 안에 넣는 것도 원하지 않는다. 그들은 날것으로 먹으면 좋은 간단한 음식인 신선한 과일과 채소, 샐러드를 자주 먹고, 만약 요리해야 한다면 완전히 익히는데 적은 시간이 드는 음식을 먹는다.

In warmer countries, on the other hand, people often prefer not to cook very much at all. They do not want the heat from an oven or fire to make their home even warmer, and they do not want to put hot food inside their body. They may choose simple food that is best eaten raw, so fresh fruit and vegetables, and salads, are often what is seen, as well as foods that, if cooked, take little time to cook through.

따뜻한 나라의 시장이나 슈퍼마켓에서는, 팔레트에 담고 싶을 만큼 다양한 색의 과일과 채소가 진열된 것을 볼 수 있고, 다양한 종류의 허브도 볼 수 있다. 햇볕이 음식에 색을 가져다준다. 한 번도 본적도, 들어 본 적도 없는 음식도 자주 있을 것이다. 그중 몇몇은 그 지역에서만 나는 다양한 종류의 생선과 함께 보일 것이다.

In the markets and supermarkets in a warm country, you will see an array of colourful fruit and vegetables to tempt your palette, as well as a big range of herbs. The sun brings colour to the foods available. There will often be foods you have never seen or heard of before. These will very often be seen alongside a variety of fish, some of which are only found in the local waters.

여행할 때는, 그 지역 음식을 먹고 즐길 수 있도록 그리고 경험하는 문화를 받아들일 수 있도록 노력해라.

When you travel, make an effort to eat and enjoy the local foods and to embrace the culture you are experiencing.

Difficult Words

1- 구매하다 – To buy/Shopping
2- 음식 – Food
3- 외국 – Foreign
4- 배움 – Learning
5- 오븐 – Oven
6- 이해하다 – To understand
7- 차가운 – Cold
8- 기름진 – Heavy
9- 태우다 – To burn
10- 위/ 배 – Stomach
11- 난방/ 온기 – Heat
12- 맛없어 보이는 – Unappetizing
13- 맛있는 – Tasty
14- 심심한 – Boring
15- 땅 속 – Underground

이야기 요약 :

외국에서 음식을 구매 하는 것은 즐겁기도 하고 방문한 국가의 문화적인 한 측면을 배울수 있는 좋은 경험이다. 추운 지방과 더운 지방의 음식 차이는 무엇이고 왜 그럴까? 이번 이야기가 이 질문들에 답변해 준다.

Summary of the Story:

Shopping for food in a foreign country is a pleasure and a learning experience on an aspect of the culture of the country visited. What is the food difference between the cold countries and warm countries and why? This story answers these questions.

Quiz:

1) 왜 더운 지방에 사는 사람들은 간단하고 날 것의 음식을 선호할까?
   a) 오랜 시간 동안 음식을 조리하는 것이 싫어서
   b) 오븐이나 불이 집 안을 덥게 하는 것이 싫어서
   c) 조리시간이 짧은 음식들만 있어서

1) Why do people in warm countries prefer to eat simple and raw food?
   a) Because they don't like to cook for hours.
   b) Because they do not want the heat from an oven or fire to make their home even warmer.
   c) Because they only have foods that take little time to cook.

2) 왜 더운지방 시장의 과일이나 야채의 색깔이 다채로울까?
   a) 햇빛이 음식의 색깔을 내어서
   b) 땅속에서 자라기 때문에
   c) 다양한 생선들과 함께 보여져서

2) Why fruits and vegetables in markets of warm country are colorful?
   a) Because the sun brings colour to the food.
   b) Because these s grows underground.
   c) Because these foods are be seen alongside a variety of fish.

3) 이 이야기의 마지막에서 권유하는 것은 무엇일까?
   a) 여행을 할 때, 당신의 문화를 공유할 음식을 가져가자.
   b) 여행을 할 때, 지역에서 잡히는 고기를 먹자.
   c) 여행을 할 때, 지역 음식을 먹고 즐기려고 노력하자.

3) What is the recommendation at the end of this story ?
   a) When you travel, bring food to share your culture.
   b) When you travel, eat the local fish.
   c) When you travel, make an effort to eat and enjoy the local foods.

ANSWERS:
   1) B
   2) A
   3) C

이야기 7: 휴가 중 바쁜 하루 (1)
STORY 7: A BUSY DAY IN THE HOLIDAYS (1)

" 아빠! 아빠! 수영하러 가도 돼요? "

"Dad! Dad! Can we go swimming?".

" 이제 잘 시간이란다. 아침에 이야기해보자. "

"It's time for bed now. We can talk about it in the morning."

지금은 학교 방학 기간이고, 나는 선생님으로서, 아들 헨리를 돌본다. 그리고 강아지 찰리도. 헨리는 8살로 활기가 넘치고 항상 분주하다. 그는 매일 밖에 나가 뭘 하고 싶어 하지만 우리는 집안일도 해야만 한다.

It's the school holidays and, as I am teacher, I look after our son, Henry. And the dog, Charlie. Henry is 8 years old and full of energy, and wants to be busy. He wants to go out and do something every day but we need to do some jobs at home as well.

그는 매일 일찍 일어나고 오늘도 예외가 아니다. 그는 곧바로 우리가 수영을 갈 수 있는지 물어본다. 나는 협상을 한다.

He gets up early every day and today is no different. He asks immediately if we can go swimming. I offer him a deal.

" 우리가 할 일을 끝내면 수영하러 갈 수 있지. 네가 좀 도와줄래? "

"We can go swimming when we have finished some jobs. Will you help me to do the jobs?"

그는 나를 쳐다보고, 여전히 확신 없이, 무슨 일을 해야 할지 걱정한다. 대답이 없자 나는 설명해준다:

He looks at me, still unsure, nervous about what he might have to do. He doesn't answer so I explain:

" 우리는 식기세척기를 비우고, 설거지하고, 세탁하고, 청소기도 돌려야 해. 이 중에서 뭐 할래? ", 나는 물었다.

"We have to empty the dishwasher, wash up, put the washing on, and hoover. Which do you want to do?", I ask him.

그는 여전히 확신하지 못하고, 다시 나를 쳐다본다.

He looks at me again, still unsure.

결국, 그는, " 그 대신 세차해도 돼요? ".

Eventually he says, "Can I wash the car instead?".

이야기 7: 휴가 중 바쁜 하루 (1)

나는 그가 제시하는 것을 잘 생각해 본다. 세차가 필요하기는 하지만 너무 쉽게 승낙하고 싶지는 않다. 나는 그가 해야만 하는 어려운 일도 있고, 보상은 스스로 얻어내야 한다는 것을 이해하길 바란다.

I think carefully about what he is offering. The car does need cleaning but I don't want to give in too easily. I want him to understand that there is hard work to do and he has to earn his treats.

나는 그가 내 차를 세차한 적이 전에 한 번 있었다는 것을 기억하지만, 그때는 나도 함께 있었다. 이번에는 그 혼자 해야 한다.

I remember that he washed my car once before, but I was with him. This time he needs to do it on his own.

나는 멈춰서 주방을 돌아보고 생각한다. 그는 계속해서 물어본다. "제발요 아빠, 대신 세차해도 돼요?".

I pause and wander around the kitchen, thinking. He asks me over and over, "Please Dad, can I wash the car instead?".

적당한 시간 후에, 나는 마지못해 동의한다. 나는 그를 차고로 데려가 양동이, 스펀지, 자동차 전용 샴푸를 찾게 하고 그에게 맡긴다.

After a reasonable pause, I give in. I take him to the garage to find the bucket, sponge and car shampoo, and leave him to it.

나는 평화롭게 라디오를 들으며 집안일을 하면서, 15분마다 그를 확인한다. 그는 열심히 하면서 맡은 일을 진지하게 받아들이고 있다.

I carry on with my jobs in the house, in peace and listening to the radio, and I check on him every 15 minutes. I see he is working hard and taking his job seriously.

그는 일을 끝내고 스펀지를 양동이에 던지면서, "아빠, 다 했어요," 라고 소리치고, 나는 확인하기 위해 밖으로 나간다.

He finishes and throws the sponge into the bucket with a shout of, "Dad, I've finished," and I go outside to check his work.

나는 차가 깨끗하게 반짝이는 것을 보고 놀라 그에게 대단한 세차 꾼이라고 말한다.

I am amazed at how clean and shiny my car is and tell him he is an amazing car cleaner.

우리는 안으로 들어가 수영복을 챙겨서 수영장으로 향한다.

We go back into the house and pack our swimming clothes, and head to the swimming pool.

수영이 끝난 후, 그는, " 정말 재밌었어요, 아빠. 내가 보상을 따낸 것 같은 느낌이에요! ".

After our swim, he says, "I really enjoyed that, Dad. I really feel as if I earned my treat!".

그리고 나는 그에게 동의한다.

And I agree with him.

이야기 7: 휴가 중 바쁜 하루 (1)

Difficult Words

1- 수영하다 – To swim
2- 침대 – Bed
3- 선생님 – Teacher
4- 개 – Dog
5- 밖에 나가다 – To go out
6- 무언가 – Something
7- 협상 – Deal
8- 확신하지 못하는 – Unsure
9- 걱정하는 – Nervous
10- 대답하다 – Answer
11- 식기세척기 – Dishwasher
12- 씻어내다 – Wash up
13- 진공청소기 – Hoover
14- 조심스럽게 – Carefully
15- 보상 – Treats/Rewards

이야기 요약 :

헨리의 방학이 시작되었다. 헨리는 8살의 혈기왕성한 아이로 항상 밖에나가 놀고 싶어하는 반면 그의 아버지는 이런저런 할 일이 많다. 오 헨리는 수영을 하겠다고 고집을 피우고, 이에 아버지는 제안을 하나 꺼낸다.

Summary of the Story:

Its school holidays and Henry, an 8-year-old energy ball, always wants to go out and do activities while his father is busy with several tasks to do. Today, Henry insists on going for a swim, so the father offers him a deal.

Quiz:

1) 아버지가 헨리에게 제안한 일 중 하나인 것은?
   a) 개에게 먹이주고 산책 시키기
   b) 식기세척기 비우기
   c) 헨리 방 치우기

1) What is one of the tasks that the father suggests Henry to do?
   a) To feed and walk the dog.
   b) To put the washing up.
   c) To clean his room.

2) 헨리가 세차를 하겠다고 했을 때 아빠가 주저한 이유는 ?
   a) 세차할 필요가 없어서
   b) 헨리 스스로 할 수 있을지 확신이 없어서
   c) 헨리가 어려운 일도 있다는 것을 깨달으며 보상받기를 원해서

2) Why did Henry's father hesitate that he washed the car?
   a) Because the car does not need cleaning.
   b) Because he is not sure if he can do it by his own.
   c) Because he wants him to understand that there is hard work to do and he has to earn his treats.

3) 이야기 마지막에서 헨리는 :
   a) 열심히 일하고 보상받은것에 행복해 했다.
   b) 수영을 더 오래 할 수 없어 슬퍼했다.
   c) 보상을 받기위해선 또 일해야 할까봐 걱정했다.

3) At the end of the story, Henry is:
   a) Happy to have worked hard and earned his treat.
   b) Sad to not be able to stay longer at the pool.
   c) Anxious to have to work again to earn a treat.

ANSWERS:
   1) B
   2) C
   3) A

이야기 8: 초콜렛 케이크
STORY 8: CHOCOLATE CAKE

케이크를 만들 때는 다음을 기억해라:
When baking cakes, remember the following:

- 케이크는 따뜻할 때 먹어라.
- Cakes are better eaten warm.
- 뜨거운 접시는 만지면 손을 델 수 있다.
- Hot dishes can burn you if you touch them.
- 재료를 신중히 계량해야 한다.
- You must measure the ingredients carefully.
- 신선할 때 즐기는 것이 더 낫다.
- It is better to enjoy them while they are fresh.

초콜릿 케이크를 만들 때 중요한 세부사항을 생각해보자.
Let's think about some important details when making a chocolate cake.

재료:
INGREDIENTS:

- 밀가루 100그램
- 설탕 100그램
- 버터 100그램
- 달걀 2개
- 초콜릿 – 진짜 초콜릿 또는 파우더
- 100 grams of flour
- 100 grams of sugar
- 100 grams of butter
- 2 eggs
- Chocolate – real chocolate or powdered

설명을 잘 따라 하면 맛있을 것이다.
If you follow the instructions carefully, it will be delicious.

1) 모든 재료를 미리 구매한 후 신선할 때 사용해라.
1) Buy all of the ingredients in advance and use them while they are still fresh.

2) 주요 재료를 매우 신중히 - 달걀, 밀가루, 버터와 설탕 - 계량하고 반죽이 부드럽고 크림 같아질 때까지 같이 섞어라. 5분에서 10분 정도 걸릴 수 있다. 버터를 미리 부드럽게 해 놓으면 더 쉽다.

2) 계 out the main ingredients - eggs, flour, butter and sugar - very carefully and then mix them together until the mixture is smooth and creamy. This may take 5 to 10 minutes. It is easier if the butter is already soft.

3) 반죽을 냉장고에서 10분 정도 식힌 후 녹은 초콜릿을 넣는다. 진짜 초콜릿을 넣는다면 아주 조심스럽게 천천히 녹인다. 초콜릿을 과열하면, 덩어리가 져서 사용할 수 없다. 녹인 초콜릿보다 파우더 초콜릿을 선호한다면, 사용하기 전에 채로 걸러 케이크 반죽에 천천히 넣는다.

3) Add the melted chocolate when the mixture has cooled in the fridge for 10 minutes. If you add real chocolate, melt it very gently and slowly. If you overheat the chocolate, it will go lumpy and you will not be able to use it.

If you prefer to add powdered chocolate instead of melted chocolate, make sure it is sieved first and then add it slowly to the cake mixture.

4) 오븐을 미리 켜 충분히 따뜻하게 해야 반죽을 구울 때 케이크가 골고루 익는다.

4) Turn on the oven so that it is warm enough when you are ready to put the mixture in to cook, and so that the cake is cooked evenly.

5) 기름을 바른 그릇(또는 그릇2개)에 반죽을 붓는다.

5) Pour the mixture into a greased dish (or 2 dishes).

6) 그릇이 준비되면 오븐에 넣는다. 20분 정도 굽는다.

6) When the dishes are ready, put them in the oven. Cook for 20 minutes.

7) 케이크가 준비되면, 그릇을 오븐에서 꺼낼 때 오븐이 너무 뜨거울 수 있으므로 손으로 만지지 않도록 주의한다. 오븐 장갑을 이용해라.

7) When the cake is ready, remember not to touch the baking dish with your hands when you take it out of the oven as it will be too hot. Use an oven glove.

8) 통에서 케이크를 꺼내놓고 식힌다.

8) Turn the cake out of its tin and leave to cool.

9) 식으면, 잘라서 즐긴다.

9) Once cool, cut a slice and enjoy.

Difficult Words

1- 케이크 – Cakes
2- 계량하다 – Measure
3- 신선한 – Fresh
4- 만들기 – Making
5- 밀가루 – Flour
6- 설탕 – Sugar
7- 버터 – Butter
8- 계란 – Egg
9- 섞다 – Mix
10- 부드러운 – Soft
11- 덩어리가 많은 – Lumpy
12- 채로 거르다 – Sieved
13- 천천히 – Slowly
14- 익혀진 – Cooked
15- 장갑 – Glove

이야기 요약 :

초콜렛 케이크를 굽기 위해선 다음 과정을 신중히 거친다. 이번 이야기에선 맛있는 초콜렛 케이크를 어떻게 준비하고 안전하게 조리하는지 그 과정을 소개한다.

Summary of the Story:

Baking a chocolate cake requires following several steps very carefully. This story tells how to prepare a delicious chocolate cake and how to cook it safely.

Quiz:

1) 케이크를 얼마 동안 구워야 하는가?

   a) 5-10 분

   b) 10 분

   c) 20 분

1) How long should the cake bake for?

   a) 5-10 minutes

   b) 10 minutes

   c) 20 minutes

2) 케이크를 오븐에서 꺼낸 뒤의 과정은 무엇인가?

   a) 케이크를 틀에서 꺼낸 뒤 식힌다.

   b) 조각을 내어 먹는다.

   c) 프로스팅을 한다.

2) What is the next step after taking the cake out of the oven ?

   a) To turn the cake out of its tin and leave to cool.

   b) To cut a slice and enjoy.

   c) To add the cake frosting.

3) 초콜렛이 과열되면 어떻게 되는가?

   a) 초콜렛이 타고, 케이크에서 탄내가 난다.

   b) 초콜렛이 지나치게 크림처럼 되어 사용할 수 없게 된다.

   c) 초콜렛이 덩어리 지게 된다.

3) What happens if you overheat the chocolate?

   a) Chocolate will burn, and the cake will have a small burn flavor.

   b) Chocolate becomes unusable because it will become too creamy.

   c) Chocolate will go lumpy.

ANSWERS:

   1) C

   2) A

   3) C

이야기 9: 스콘을 굽는 방법
STORY 9: HOW TO BAKE SCONES

스콘은 차 마시는 시간에 곁들이는 영국의 대표적인 빵으로, 쉽게 만들 수 있다. 이 스콘 조리법은 다른 맛이나 속 재료를 원한다면 바꾸기도 쉽다.

Scones are a classic English tea-time treat and are very easy to make. This scone recipe is also easy to change if you want to try a different flavour or filling.

재료:

INGREDIENTS:

- 베이킹파우더가 든 밀가루 225g
- 소금 한 자밤
- 소프트 버터 55g
- 정제당 25g
- 우유 150mL
- 코팅하기 위해 푼 방목 달걀 1개(약간의 우유도 대체로 가능하다).

- 225g of self-raising flour
- a pinch of salt
- 55g of soft butter
- 25g of caster sugar
- 150ml of milk
- 1 free-range egg, beaten, to glaze (although you could, alternatively, use a little milk).

방법:

METHOD:

1) 오븐을 200 °C로 예열한다.
1) Heat the oven to 200°C.

2) 제빵 시트에 얇게 기름을 칠하거나, 기름이 배지 않는 종이를 놓는다.
2) Lightly grease a baking sheet, or put a piece of greaseproof paper on it.

3) 밀가루와 소금을 함께 섞은 후, 부드러워진 버터에 섞는다.
3) Mix together the flour and salt, then rub in the softened butter.

4) 설탕을 조금씩 넣어주며 섞고, 부드러운 반죽을 만들기 위해 우유를 넣는다.
4) Stir in the sugar, a little at a time, and then add the milk to make a soft dough.

5) 그릇 안에서 손으로 반죽하고, 밀가루를 칠한 반죽대 위에서 다시 가볍게 반죽한다.

5) Work the mixture well with your hands in the mixing bowl, then turn it out onto a floured surface and knead it again lightly.

6) 반죽을 살살 펴 대략 2cm 두께로 동그랗게 만든다. 5cm 커터를 사용해 동그란 모양으로 자르고 / 스콘을 하나씩 제빵 시트 위에 놓는다.

6) Pat out the mixture into a round shape roughly 2cm thick. Use a 5cm cutter to make rounds / individual scones, and place them on the baking sheet.

7) 반죽에서 남은 부분을 가져와 6번을 반복한다. 모든 반죽을 스콘으로 만드는데 다 쓸 때까지 계속한다.

7) Pull together what is left of the dough and repeat Step 6. Keep doing this until you have used all of the mixture to make scones.

8) 풀어 놓은 달걀 물을 스콘 윗부분에 바른다(또는 우유로). 제빵 시트를 오븐에 넣는다.

8) Brush the tops of the scones with the beaten egg (or the milk). Put the baking sheet in the oven.

9) 반죽이 잘 부풀어 오르고 겉면이 황금빛이 될 때까지 12에서 15분 정도 굽는다.

9) Bake for between 12 and 15 minutes until well risen and golden on the top.

10) 선반에서 식힌 후 버터와 좋은 잼(딸기잼이 잘 어울린다)과 함께 내놓거나 버터 대신에 고형 크림을 곁들여도 좋다.

10) Cool on a wire rack and serve with butter and a good jam (strawberry works very well), or maybe some clotted cream instead of the butter.

4번에서 말린 과일을 넣어 요리법을 바꿀 수도 있다. 육두구나 시나몬 같은 향신료를 첨가할 수도 있다.

You can change the recipe by adding dried fruit at Step 4. You can also add some spices such as nutmeg or cinnamon.

설탕은 남겨두고 100g의 치즈를 갈아 넣어 치즈(짭짤한) 스콘을 만들 수도 있다. 체더치즈처럼 강한 치즈가 잘 어울린다.

You can make cheese (savoury) scones by leaving out the sugar and adding 100 grams of grated cheese. A strong cheese such as cheddar works best.

맛있게 드세요!

Enjoy!

Difficult Words

1- 조리법 – Recipe
2- 맛/ 풍미 – Flavor
3- 속재료 – Filling
4- 베이킹파우더가 든 – Self raising
5- 우유 – Milk
6- 잘 풀어진 – Beaten
7- 코팅하다 – To glaze
8- 유산지 – Baking sheet
9- 반죽하다 – To knead
10- 잼 – Jam
11- 반죽 – Mixture
12- 향신료 – Spices
13- 치즈 – Cheese
14- 시나몬 – Cinnamon
15- 육두구 – Nutmeg

이야기 요약 :

이번 이야기는 스콘을 어떻게 굽는지, 그 재료들과 다양한 맛을 얻기 위한 여러 방법들을 소개한다.

Summary of the Story:

This story describes how to cook scones, its ingredients and the different options for obtaining scones with different flavors.

Quiz:

1) 계란 대신 사용할 수 있는 재료는?

   a) 우유

   b) 정제 설탕

   c) 부드럽게 된 버터

1) What ingredient can you use instead of the egg?

   a) Milk

   b) caster sugar

   c) Soft Butter

2) 스콘을 오븐에 굽는 시간은 얼마인가요?

   a) 8 에서 10분

   b) 12 에서 15 분

   c) 20분, 윗부분이 부풀어 오르고 잘 구어진 색이 돌 때까지

2) What is the cooking time of the scones in the oven?

   a) 8 to 10 minutes

   b) 12 to 15 minutes

   c) 20 minutes, until well risen and golden on the top

3) 다음 중 스콘에 사용할 수 없는 재료는?

   a) 잼

   b) 응고된 크림

   c) 초콜렛

3) Which of these ingredients is not recommended to be used with scones?

   a) Jam

   b) Clotted cream

   c) Chocolate

ANSWERS:

   1) A

   2) B

   3) C

이야기 10: 인터넷
STORY 10: INTERNET

현대 기술의 출현과 함께, 오늘날의 사람들은 이전 세대보다 좀 더 편리하고 편안한 삶을 즐길 수 있다.

With the advent of modern technology, people today can enjoy more convenient and comfortable lives compared to the older generations.

이런 정보화 시대에, 가진 편리함과 잠재력 때문에 구글이나 사파리, 빙같은 검색엔진이 가장 널리 사용되는 컴퓨터 응용프로그램 중 하나이다.

In this Information Age, search engines such as Google, Safari and Bing are amongst the most widely used computer applications because of their convenience and potential.

기본적인 컴퓨터 기술만 가지고도 사람들은 문제에 대한 해답을 쉽게 찾으면서 동시에 그들의 호기심도 충족할 수 있다.

With only basic computer skills, people can easily find answers to their problems at the same time as satisfying their curiosity.

많은 학생이 학습적인 목적으로 검색 엔진을 남용한다. 그들은 가끔 검색 엔진에만 의존해 정보를 찾고, 책을 읽거나 다른 학생과의 대화 같은 다른 정보는 탐색하지 않는다. 그들은 쉽게 호기심에 대한 감각을 잃을 수 있다.

Many students make excessive use of search engines for academic purposes. They sometimes rely solely on search engines for their information and do not explore other sources of information, such as reading books or engaging in conversations with their fellow students. They can easily lose their sense of curiosity.

현명한 학생들은 공개된 온라인 자료보다 현실에서 정보를 모으는데 시간을 더 투자해 더욱 독특하고, 개성 있으며 흥미로운 대답을 찾아낸다.

Wise students spend more time gathering their information from the real world rather than public, online sources and so come up with more unique, individual, and interesting answers.

컴퓨터와 기술은 사람들의 삶에 중요한 역할을 하지만, 그들의 사생활에 영향을 줄 수도 있다.

Computers and technology do play a vital role in peoples' lives, but they can also affect their privacy.

범죄자들이 개인 정보를 쉽게 볼 수 있고, 개인이 컴퓨터 사용에 대해 심각하게 받아들이지 않을수록 위험은 더 커진다.

It is easy for criminals to see an individual's information and the risk of this is greater if an individual does not think seriously about how they use their computer.

사생활침해는 디지털 시대에 불가피한 일처럼 보이지만, 그래서는 안 된다. 예전에는 허가 없이 누군가의 은행 정보나 생일, 주민등록번호를 아는 것이 거의 불가능했었다. 하지만 오늘날에는 이런 정보를 찾아내기가 쉬워 보인다.

*참고: Social security number (사회 보장 번호) 는 미국의 주민등록번호의 개념으로 사용됩니다.

Invasion of privacy may seem inevitable in this digital age, but it should not be. It used to be almost impossible to find out somebody's bank details, date of birth, or social security number, without their permission. But today, these details seem to be so easy to find out.

소셜 네트워킹 웹사이트들은 범죄나 악의가 있는 목적에 사용하려는 사람들에게 유용한 정보인 개인의 사생활에 대한 정보를 나누도록 부추긴다. 사람들은 태생적으로 다른 사람들과 어울리기를 좋아해서 그들의 경험을 나누고 싶어 하지만, 이렇게 기술을 사용하는 것이 그들의 삶에 문제를 일으킬 수 있다.

Social networking sites encourage people to be open about their private lives and to share information that is useful to others who wish to use it for criminal or malicious purposes. People are naturally sociable and want to share their experiences, but doing so through the use of technology can cause them problems in their lives.

개인은 그들의 삶과 컴퓨터 사용을 통제할 수 있고, 여기에 인터넷이 중요한 부분을 차지한다.

Individuals can take control of their lives and how they use their computer and the Internet is a significant part of this.

Difficult Words

1- 출현 – Advent
2- 오래 된 – Older
3- 검색 엔진 – Search engines
4- 편리한 – Convenience
5- 기술들 – Skills
6- 학생들 – Students
7- 현명한 – Wises
8- 독특한 – Uniques
9- 디지털 세대 – Digital age
10- 생년월일 – Date of birth
11- 허가 – Permission
12- 소셜 네트워킹 – Social networking sites
13- 공유하다 – To share
14- 은행 정보 – Bank details
15- 사회 보장 번호 – Social security number

이야기 요약 :

인터넷은 기술의 세계를 혁명적으로 변화시켰다. 오늘날 사람들은 그 편리성과 잠재성 때문에 매일 인터넷을 사용한다. 우리는 이전 세대보다 더 편리한 삶을 즐기고 있지만, 인터넷으로 인해 그 이전 세대들은 겪지 않은 방면에 부정적인 영향을 경험하고 있다.

Summary of the Story:

Internet has revolutionized the world of technology. Now, people use it daily because of its convenience and potential. They can enjoy a more comfortable life than previous generations, but Internet also brings negative aspects to which previous generations could not have been victims.

Quiz:

1) 학생들이 학구 목적으로 검색 엔진만을 사용할때 생기는 부정적인 결과로 언급되지 않은 것은 ?

   a) 호기심을 잃게 된다.

   b) 질문에 대한 답을 쉽게 찾기 때문에 학생들이 덜 똑똑해 진다.

   c) 책이나 다른 정보 출처에서 얻을 수 있는 독창적이고 개인적이며 개인화 된 답을 더 이상 찾지 못한다.

1) Which of these consequences is not mentioned when students rely solely on search engines for academic purposes?

   a) Students can easily lose their sense of curiosity.

   b) Students become less intelligent because they find the answers to their questions too easily.

   c) Students no longer find original, individual and personalized answers that can be found in books and other sources of information.

2) 이전 세대에는 불가능 했으나 현재는 찾기 쉬어진 정보는?

   a) 생년월일, 은행정보, 사회 보장 번호와 같은 개인 정보

   b) 전화번호

   c) 거주지 주소

2) What information is now easy to find due to the internet that was not available in previous generations?

   a) Personal information such as date of birth, bank details and social security number.

   b) Phone number.

   c) Residence addresse.

3) 소셜 네트워킹의 주된 단점은?

   a) 개인 사생활을 공개하고 공유하도록 조장하고, 그 정보들이 범죄나 악의적인 목적에 사용하기를 원하는 사람들에게 악용될 수 있다.

   b) 젊은 세대의 시간을 소비하여 덜 생산적이 된다.

   c) 자신의 삶을 남의 것과 비교하여 젊은 층의 우울감 수준이 증가한다.

3) What is the main negative aspect of social networking?

   a) It encourages people to be open about their private lives and to share information that is useful to others who wish to use it for criminal or malicious purposes.

   b) It consumes the time of the younger generations and they are becoming less productive.

   c) It compares our lives with those of others and increase the level of depression in young people.

ANSWERS:

   1) B

   2) A

   3) A

이야기 11: 해협 터널
STORY 11: CHANNEL TUNNEL

만약 당신이 차로 영국과 유럽을 여행하고 싶다면, 채널 터널을 통해 여행하는 것이 쉬운 방법이 된다.

If you want to travel by car between Britain and Europe, travelling through the Channel Tunnel is the easy way to do it.

고속도로를 이용해 그곳에 가는 것이 쉽고 표지판 또한 잘 설치되어 있다.

Getting there on the motorway is very straightforward and it is well-signposted.

일단 도착하면, 간단하고 순조롭게 진행된다.

Once you arrive, it is a simple process and it usually goes smoothly.

만약 예약하면, 자동 요금소를 이용할 수 있다. 간단히 예약 번호를 입력한다. 기차가 정시에 도착하는지 볼 수 있고 (정시에 출발하지 않는다면) 몇 시에 출발할 수 있는지도 볼 수 있다. 예약을 통해, 유로터널은 당신이 예약한 기차로 여행할 수 있도록 보장해준다. 예약한 출발 시각보다 45분 일찍 도착하는 것을 권장하며, 바쁜 여름 시즌에는 여유 있게 가는 것이 좋다.

If you have pre-booked, you can use an automatic toll booth. You simply enter your booking reference number. You will see if your train is running on time and, if not, what time you can depart. With pre-booking, Eurotunnel does all that it can to ensure you travel on the train you have booked. You are advised to arrive 45 minutes ahead of your pre-booked departure time, although allow plenty of time during the busy summer months.

예약하지 않을 경우, 도착해서 비용을 지급할 수 있다. 이 방법으로, 자리가 있는 다음 기차로 여행할 수 있다.

If you have not pre-booked, you can pay when you arrive. With this option, you travel on the next train that has a space.

어떤 방법이든, 차에 걸어 둘 코드명을 받을 것이다. 코드명을 기억해라!

Either way, you will be given a letter code to hang in your car. Remember your code!

요금소를 지나면, 터미널에 들어간다. 화장실을 가거나 마지막으로 잊고 있던 물건을 사러 가게에 가는 것이 좋다. 다양한 향수나 전자제품, 술, 사탕 종류를 파는 가게뿐 아니라 먹을 수 있는 장소도 많다.

After the toll booth, you go through to the terminal. It's always useful to visit the toilet and to check the shops for any last-minute items you have forgotten. There is a range of shops offering perfume, electrical items, alcohol and sweets, as well as a number of places to eat.

어떤 기차가 지금 들어오는지, 어떤 코드가 저 기차와 관련 있는지는 스크린을 보면 알 수 있다. 또한, 언제 당신의 코드가 불릴지도 알려준다. 이는 내가 커피를 마시거나 다른 것을 할 시간이 있는지 아는 데 도움이 된다.

Look at the screens to find out which train is loading currently and which letter code relates to that train. They also let you know when your letter is likely to be called. This helps you to know if you have time for a coffee or something more.

당신의 코드가 불리면, 차로 돌아가서 신호를 따른다. 기차로 오를 행렬에 들어가기 전, 출입국 관리와 보안 검색을 지날 것이다.

When your letter is called, return to your car and follow the signs. You will go through passport control and then through a security area, before joining the queue to drive on to the train.

이 줄은 엄격하게 관리되므로 행동에 주의하며 줄 안쪽에서 기다린다.

These queues are closely managed and you must behave yourself and wait in line.

기차에 오를 차례가 되면, 내부가 꽤 작고 좁으므로 조심히 운전하여 천천히 기차에 들어간다. 안내직원이 주차하라고 할 때까지 앞으로 나아간다.

When you are called to board the train, drive carefully and enter the train slowly as it is quite small and narrow inside. Proceed until a member of staff tells you to park.

주차할 때 나오는 보안 정보를 주의 깊게 들어야 한다. 지시를 따르는 것은 자신의 안전과 다른 여행자들에게도 매우 중요하다. 예를 들어, 플래시 촬영은 금지된다.

When you park, you must listen carefully to the security information you hear. It is very important that you follow the instructions – for your own safety and that of the other travellers. For example, flash photography is not allowed.

건너는 동안 차 옆에서 기다리도록 지시받으며, 창문은 열어 두어야 한다.

You are advised to wait by your car during the crossing, and must leave a car window open.

차량에서는 보안 검사가 있고 여정을 시작하기 위해 엔진이 가동되는 것이 들릴 것이다. 여정 자체는 35분밖에 걸리지 않으며, 시간은 금방 간다.

There are security checks on the vehicle and then you will hear the engines getting ready to start the journey. The journey itself lasts only 35 minutes, and the time flies by.

몇몇 운전자들은 자신의 여행을 계속하기 전 이 시간을 잠자는 데 이용한다. 다른 사람들은 간식을 먹거나 게임을 하는 데 시간을 보낸다.

Some drivers use this time to sleep before continuing their onward journey. Others use the time to eat a snack or to play games.

건너편에 도착하면, 문을 열고 운전하기 전에 보안 검사가 더 있다.

When you reach the other side, there are more security checks before they open the doors and you drive away.

채널 터널을 통해 여행하기는 아주 쉽다.

Travelling through the Channel Tunnel is so easy.

Difficult Words

1- 그곳에 가는 것 – Getting there
2- 표지판이 잘 설치된 – Well-signposted
3- 순조롭게 – Smoothly
4- 진행 – Process
5- 보통 – Usually
6- 요금소 – Toll booth
7- 예약 – Booking
8- 지시받은 – Advised
9- 자리 – Space
10- 다음 – Next
11- 잊고 있던 – Have forgotten
12- 사탕류 – Sweets
13- 따르다 – Follow
14- 줄 – Queue
15- 관리되다 – Managed

이야기 요약 :

해협 터널은 유럽과 영국을 여행하는 가장 빠르고 쉬운 길이다. 이번 이야기에선 이 터널을 순조롭게 통과하기 위한 과정을 설명하였다.

Summary of the Story:

The Channel Tunnel is the quickest and easiest way to travel between Europe and Britain. This story describes the process to get through this tunnel smoothly.

Quiz:

1) 사전 예약이 되 있다면 얼마나 미리 도착해 있어야 하는가?
   a) 35 분
   b) 45 분
   c) 1 시간

1) How long in advance should you arrive when you have a pre-booked?
   a) 35 minutes
   b) 45 minutes
   c) 1 hour

2) 터미널에서 찾아볼 수 있는 것은?
   a) 레스토랑
   b) 비디오 게임
   c) 바

2) What can be found in the terminal?
   a) Restaurants
   b) Video games
   c) bars

3) 건너가는 동안 당신이 해야 할 것은 :
   a) 가게들을 돌아다니는 것
   b) 편안히 휴식하며 커피를 즐기는 것
   c) 자신의 차 옆에서 기다리기

3) During the crossing, you are advised to :
   a) To wander in the shops.
   b) To relax and get a coffee.
   c) To wait next to your car.

ANSWERS:
   1) A
   2) A
   3) C

이야기 12: 일기예보
STORY 12: WEATHER REPORT

앞으로 12시간 동안의 일기예보입니다.

Here is the country's forecast for the next 12 hours.

오늘 북쪽 지방은 춥고 습하겠습니다. 많은 비가 올 것으로 예상되는 가운데 정오부터 오후 4시 사이에 10cm 이하의 비가 내리겠으며 진눈깨비와 우박의 피해도 주의하셔야겠습니다. 예년보다 기온이 낮고, 밤에는 서리의 피해도 예상됩니다. 운전에 특히 주의하시고 빙판 도로에 주의하십시오.

In the north of the country today, it is cold and wet. Heavy rain is forecast, with up to 10cm falling between midday and 1600, and there is also a risk of sleet and hail. The temperature is low for the time of year and, as night falls, there is a risk of frost. Take extra care if you are driving, and look out for ice on the roads.

서쪽 지역은 아침에는 온화한 날씨를 보이겠으나, 오후에 들어서면 여전히 비가 올 가능성이 있습니다. 비가 오면 천둥·번개, 강한 바람을 동반한 폭풍과 강풍에 대비하시기 바랍니다. 우산을 챙기시더라도 천둥소리가 들리거나 번개가 보이면 사용하지 마시고 애완동물은 실내에서 보호하시기 바랍니다! 저녁에는 비가 오지는 않지만 바람이 불고 기온이 올라가 정상적인 예년 기온을 보이겠습니다.

The west of the country is looking fair in the morning, but there is still a high risk of rain, especially in the afternoon. Be prepared for some storms if it rains, with strong winds, some gale force, and thunder and lightning. Take an umbrella but remember not to use it if you hear thunder or see lightning, and keep your pets indoors! The evening is dry but still windy, with temperatures rising so that they are normal for the time of year.

동쪽 지역은 특히 아침에 안개가 끼고 흐린 날씨를 보이겠습니다. 습하고 시원하겠으나 비 때문은 아닙니다. 서쪽에서 불어오는 강풍에 주의하십시오. 예년과 비슷한 기온을 보이겠으며 서쪽에서 오는 폭풍은 동쪽에 닿기 전에 잦아들겠습니다.

The east of the country is expected to be foggy or misty, especially in the morning. It feels damp, and therefore cool, but it is not due to rain at all. Beware of strong winds, some gale force, coming from the west. The temperatures are normal for the time of year and the storms in the west will die out before reaching the east.

남쪽 지역은 날씨가 좋겠습니다. 가벼운 바람과 따뜻한 기온으로, 비 소식은 없겠습니다. 예년보다 강수량은 계속 낮고 기온은 높겠습니다. 기온이 높으니 외출하실 때는 물을 챙겨나가세요. 애완동물과 아이들은 햇볕에 타지 않게 주의하시고 탈수에도 주의하시기 바랍니다.

The south of the country is enjoying fine weather. There is a light breeze and warm temperatures, with no risk of rain. Rainfall in the south continues to be low for the time of year, with the temperatures high for the time of year. Because of the high temperatures, make sure you take water with you when you go out. Make sure your pets and children are not at risk of getting sunburn or dehydrated.

내일 일기예보는 맑고 건조한 것으로 보입니다.

The forecast for tomorrow looks fine and dry.

Difficult Words

1- 예보 – Forecast
2- 습하다 – Wet
3- 비 – Rain
4- 진눈깨비 – Sleet
5- 우박 – Hail
6- 밤 – Night
7- 서리 – Frost
8- 주의 – Care
9- 햇볕에 탐 – Sunburn
10- 폭풍우 – Storms
11- 천둥 – Thunder
12- 번개 – Lightning
13- 바람이 많이 부는 – Windy
14- 건조한 – Dry
15- 안개가 낀 – Foggy

줄거리 요약 :

이번 이야기는 동서남북의 날씨 상황과 해당 국가 사람들에게 권고사항을 설명하고 있다.

Summary of the Story:

This story describes the weather in the north, south, east and west of a country with recommendations for the people of that country.

Quiz:

1) 왜 운전자들이 북쪽 지역 운전을 조심해야 하는가?
   a) 도로에 서리 위험이 있을 수 있어서
   b) 폭우 위험이 있어서
   c) 짙은 안개가 예상 되어서

1) Why drivers should be careful in the north part of the country?
   a) Because there is risk of frost on the road.
   b) Because a heavy rain is forecasted.
   c) Because there will be a lot of frog on the roads.

2) 남쪽 지방에 사는 사람들에게 권고하는 사항은?
   a) 우산을 가지고 다니되, 천둥번개시 사용하지 말 것
   b) 햇볕에 의한 화상을 조심하고 자주 물을 마실 것
   c) 바람이 거세므로 가축들을 실내에 둘 것

2) What is the advice for the people living in the south of the country?
   a) Bring your umbrella, but don't use it if there is thunder or lightning.
   b) Avoid sun burn and stay hydrated.
   c) Keep the animals inside, because wind will be strong.

3) 동부지방의 기온은 어떠한가?
   a) 예년에 비해 높다.
   b) 예년에 비해 낮다.
   c) 예년과 비슷하다.

3) What is the temperature in the east of the country?
   a) The temperature is high for the time of year.
   b) The temperature is low for the time of year.
   c) The temperatures are normal for the time of year.

ANSWERS:
   1) A
   2) B
   3) C

이야기 13: 휴가 중 바쁜 하루(2)
STORY 13: A BUSY DAY IN THE HOLIDAYS (2)

헨리와 나는 어떻게 일이 - 그리고 직업이 - 원하는 것이나 심지어 돈을 버는 것을 돕는지 이야기한다. 그는 세차하고 그 보상으로 수영하러 갔던 것을 기억한다.

Henry and I talk about how working - and doing jobs - helps you to earn treats or, perhaps, money. He remembers cleaning the car and being taken swimming as his reward.

그는 일어나서 - 활력이 넘치고 언제나처럼 분주하게 - 오늘은 무엇을 할 지 물어본다.

He gets up – full of energy and wanting to be busy, as always – and asks what jobs he can do today.

아침 식사 후에, 우리는 그가 정말로 무슨 일을 할 수 있을지 그의 키를 고려하여 생각해본다. 그러고 나서 오늘 해야 할 일을 이야기한다.

After breakfast, we start by thinking about what he can ☐ do, given his size. Then we talk about what needs to be done today.

나는 마을 안 식료품 가게에서 우유와 빵을 사야 한다고 말한다. 헨리는 잔디를 깎아야 하고 강아지를 산책시켜야 한다고 말한다. 나는 화장실 대청소가 필요하고 집 안을 청소기로 청소해야 할 필요가 있다고 말한다.

I say we need some milk and bread from the grocery store in the village. Henry says the lawn needs mowing and we must walk the dog. I mention that the bathroom needs a good clean and the house need to be hoovered.

우리는 헨리가 강아지를 데리고 식료품 가게에 가서, 강아지를 밖에 묶어 놓고, 우유와 빵을 사러 들어가는 것에 찬성한다. 그는 흥분한 강아지와 함께 경쾌한 발걸음으로 출발한다. 나는 고무장갑과 청소 용품을 찾아 화장실 청소할 준비를 한다. 이 일이 제일 하기 싫은 일이지만, 헨리를 시킬 수는 없다. 청소가 끝나고, 벽장에서 진공청소기를 꺼내어 집 안을 청소한다. 끝나고 나니 구석구석이 모두 훨씬 더 깨끗하게 보이는 것 같이 느껴진다.

We agree that Henry can walk the dog to the grocery store, tie him up outside, then go in and buy the milk and the bread. He sets off with an excited dog and a spring in his step. I find the rubber gloves and cleaning products, and set to cleaning the bathroom. This is the job I like the least, but I can't ask Henry to do it. When I finish, I then take the hoover from the cupboard and hoover around the house. Everywhere looks and feels much cleaner when I finish.

헨리가 우유, 빵, 강아지 그리고 나중에 우리가 모두 먹을 초콜릿 바를 사서 집에 왔다. 아주 좋은 생각이다!

Henry comes home with the milk and the bread, and the dog, and a bar of chocolate for each of us to have later. Great idea!

잔디는 함께 깎기로 한다. 시간이 좀 걸린다. 내가 잔디 깎기를 밀고 헨리가 잘린 풀을 갈퀴로 긁어낸다. 그는 눈에 안 띄는 구석에 잡초더미를 만든다.

We decide to mow the lawn together. It takes a while. I push the mower and Henry rakes up the grass cuttings. He puts them in a pile in the corner, out of the way.

이제 점심시간이 가까워져 오고 우리는 일을 거의 끝냈다. 헨리가 식탁을 차리고 나는 샌드위치를 만든다. 우리는 함께 앉아서 점심을 먹는다.

It's almost lunch time and we have almost finished our jobs. Henry sets the table and I make us a sandwich. We sit down to eat lunch together.

우리는 오후에 무엇을 할지 결정하려다가 둘 다 너무 피곤하니 집에서 쉬며 우리가 한 일을 감상하기로 한다. 물론, 초콜릿도 먹으면서.

We try to decide what to do in the afternoon and agree that we are both too tired and just want to stay at home and relax, and admire our work. And eat our chocolate, of course.

또 다른 아주 좋은 생각이다!

Another great idea!

Difficult Words

1- 바쁜 – Busy
2- 언제나 – Always
3- 정말로 – Actally
4- 빵 – Bread
5- 잔디 – Lawn
6- 잔디깎기 – Mowing
7- 묶다 – To tie
8- 고무장갑 – Robber gloves
9- 벽장 – Cupboard
10- 청소기 – Cleaner
11- 좋은 생각 – Great idea
12- 함께 – Together
13- 잔디 – Grass
14- 구석 – Corner
15- 피곤한 – Tired

이야기 요약 :

헨리는 8살 소년으로, 보상을 받기위해 일을한다는 개념을 좋아한다. 헨리와 헨리의 아버지는 그날 해야할 일들을 함께 결정하는 기회를 가진다.

Summary of the Story:

Henry, an energetic 8-year-old boy, now loves the concept of working in return for reward. He and his father take the opportunity to decide together on the tasks to be carried out for the day.

Quiz:

1) 헨리가 식료품점에 다녀오는 동안 헨리의 아버지는 무엇을 했나?
   a) 잔디깎이
   b) 화장실 청소
   c) 편히 쉬며 초콜렛을 먹음

1) What does Henry's father do while Henry's going to the grocery store?
   a) He mows the lawn.
   b) He cleans the bathroom.
   c) He relaxes and eats chocolate.

2) 누가 진공청소기를 밀었나?
   a) 헨리
   b) 헨리 아버지
   c) 아무도 하지 않음

2) Who is vacuuming?
   a) Henry
   b) Henry's father
   c) No one is doing the vacuum.

3) 하루중 언제 그 둘의 일이 마쳐졌나 ?
   a) 아침
   b) 오후 늦게
   c) 점심시간 즈음

3) What time of the day does Henry and his father finish working?
   a) In morning
   b) At the end of the afternoon
   c) Around lunch time

ANSWERS:
   1) B
   2) B
   3) C

이야기 14: 스마트폰
STORY 14: SMARTPHONES

애플사에 의해 스마트폰이 개발된 지 십 년이 지났다. 휴대전화는 그 이전에도 많았지만, 스마트폰은 우리가 서로 대화하는 수단을 바꿔놓는다.

It is just over a decade since the smartphone was invented by Apple. Mobile phones were common enough before then but the smartphone changes how we communicate with each other.

휴대전화 음성통화 수가 2017년 처음으로 하락했다 - 우리가 기기에 단단히 빠져있음에도 불구하고 말이다.

The number of voice calls made on mobile phones fell for the first time in 2017 - despite the fact we are hooked on our devices.

성인의 78%가 스마트폰을 가지고 있다.

A total of 78% of all adults now owns a smartphone.

평균적으로, 우리는 일어나 12분마다 한 번씩 휴대전화를 확인한다고 한다.

On average, it is believed that people check their phone once every 12 minutes when they're awake.

다섯 명 중 두 명은 일어나서 5분 안에 휴대전화를 보고, 3분의 1은 잠들기 직전까지 휴대전화를 확인한다.

Two in five adults look at their phone within five minutes of waking up, and a third check their phones just before falling asleep.

높은 퍼센트 (71%)의 사람들은 절대로 휴대전화를 꺼놓지 않는다고 하고 78%는 휴대전화 없이는 살 수 없다고 공공연히 말한다.

It is understood that a high percentage (71%) of people never turn off their phone and 78% openly say they cannot live without it.

75%의 사람들은 아직도 음성 통화를 휴대전화의 가장 중요한 기능으로 여기고, 더 많은 (92%) 사람들은 웹 탐색을 중요하다고 믿고 휴대전화도 이 기능에 맞춰 고른다.

*참고: Three-quarters는 4분의 3이라는 뜻으로 4명 중 3명의 사람, 즉 75%의 사람들의 비율을 말하고 있다.

Three-quarters of people still regard voice calling as an important function of their phones, more (92%) believe web browsing is crucial, and they choose to use their phone to do this.

휴대 전화상의 전체 통화 기록은 전화를 거는데 드는 비용이 (예전과 비교해) 최저임에도 불구하고 2017년 1.7% 정도 하락했다.

It is believed that the total number of calls made on mobiles fell by 1.7% in 2017, even though making them is the cheapest it has ever been.

그 말은 사람들이 서로 대화를 더 적게 한다는 뜻이라기보다는, 다른 방법으로 대화한다는 뜻이다.

That does not necessarily mean people are talking to each other less, but they are talking in different ways.

지난 십 년간, 스마트폰의 증가로 인해 사람들의 삶이 달라졌고 인터넷과 새로운 서비스로의 접근 또한 쉬워졌다. 우리는 그 어느 때 보다 이동 중에 더 많은 일을 할 수 있게 되었다.

It is agreed that, over the last decade, people's lives have been transformed by the rise of the smartphone, together with better access to the internet and new services. We can do more on the move than ever before.

사람들은 스마트폰을 그들의 충실한 동반자로 생각하지만, 어떤 사람들은 온라인상에서 과부하가 걸린 듯한 느낌을 받고 온라인상이 아닐 때면 좌절감을 느낀다고 한다.

People agree their smartphone is their constant companion, but some are finding themselves overloaded when online, or frustrated when they're not.

가족 내에서도, 가족 구성원들은 서로 다른 이유로 스마트폰에 의존한다. 한 사람은 소셜 미디어나 날씨를 확인하거나 쇼핑 리스트를 저장하는 데 스마트폰을 사용한다면, 다른 사람은 택시를 부르거나 이메일을 읽는 데 사용할 것이다. 나머지 다른 사람들은 게임을 하거나 인터넷 검색, 유튜브 채널을 보는 것에 사용한다.

Within families, different members depend on their smartphones for different reasons. One may use it for checking social media and the weather, and to store shopping lists; another will use it to book taxis and read emails. Others use it to play games, search the internet, and watch YouTube.

그리고 어떤 가족들은 스마트폰을 사용하는 것이 언제 공손하고, 언제 보이지 않도록 해야 하는지에 대한 규칙이 있다.

And some families have rules for when it is polite to use a smartphone and when it should be kept out of sight.

언제 어디에서 휴대전화를 사용할 것인지 규칙을 정한 적이 있는가?

Have you set any rules for when and where you use your phone?

Difficult Words

1- 10년 – Decade
2- 음성통화 – Voice Calls
3- 평균 – Average
4- 깨어 있는 – Awake
5- 일어난 상태 – Waking up
6- 잠들기 – Falling asleep
7- 높은 – High
8- 공공연히 – Openly
9- 살다 – To live
10- 탐색 – Browsing
11- 중요한 – Crucial
12- 하락하다 – Fell
13- 과부하가 걸린 – Overload
14- 날씨 – Weather
15- 쇼핑 리스트, 구매 목록 – Shopping lists

이야기 요약 :

애플사에 의해 스마트폰이 개발된 지도 10년이 지났다. 비록 이 발명 전에도 휴대전화는 있었지만, 스마트폰은 우리가 소통하는 방식을 바꿔놓았다. 이번 이야기에선 오늘날 스마트폰 사용에 관한 연구 결과를 설명한다.

Summary of the Story:

It has now been over a decade since the smartphone was invented by Apple. Even if cellphones existed before this invention, smartphones are changing the way we communicate with each other. This story describes the results of a study on the use of smartphones today.

Quiz:

1) 평균적으로 얼마나 자주 사람들은 스마트폰을 확인하는가?

   a) 약 5분 마다

   b) 약 12분 마다

   c) 약 15분 마다

1) On average, how often do people check their phone?

   a) Around every 5 minutes

   b) Around every 12 minutes

   c) Around every 15 minutes

2) 일어나자마자 프마트 폰을 확인하는 성인의 비율은?

   a) 5명 중 2명

   b) 5명 중 3명

   c) 5명 중 1명

2) What is the percentage of adults who checks their phone the moment they wake up?

   a) Two in five adults

   b) Three in five adults

   c) One in five adults

3) 다음 진술 중 옳은 것은?

   a) 오직 25% 정도의 사람들만이 음성통화가 전화기의 가장 중요한 기능이라고 생각한다.

   b) 75%이상의 사람이 인터넷 탐색이 가장 중요한 기능이라고 여긴다.

   c) 전화에서는, 음성 통화가 웹을 검색하는 것보다 더 중요하게 여겨진다.

3) Which of these statements is true?

   a) Only a quarter of people still consider voice calls an important function of their phones.

   b) More than three-quarters of people consider web browsing to be crucial.

   c) On phones, voice calling is considered more important than browsing the web.

ANSWERS:

   1) B

   2) A

   3) B

이야기 15: 체스터
STORY 15: CHESTER

체스터는 체셔(Cheshire) 주의 수도로, 영국의 서북부 지역에 위치해 웨일스(Welsh) 국경과 아주 가깝다. 몇몇 영국 사람들은 체스터가 영국에 있는지 아니면 웨일스에 있는지 잘 모르지만, 확실히 영국에 있다.

Chester is the county town of Cheshire, which is in the north-west of England, very close to the Welsh border. Some British people are uncertain whether Chester is in England or Wales, but it is definitely in England.

주 수도이자 거의 2,000년 동안 도시로 존재해 왔다.

As well as being the county town, it has been a city for nearly 2,000 years.

체스터는 로마 도시로 오늘날에도 여전히 많은 로마 유적을 볼 수 있다. 가장 중요한 유적은 영국에서 가장 온전히 보존된 성곽인 시티월스(the City Walls)이다. 성곽 주변을 쉽게 걸을 수 있고 이는 최초의 요새에 설치된 벽이었다. 3km 정도의 길이로 초기의 마을을 감싸고 있다. 서기 70년에서 서기 80년 사이에 지어졌다. 로마 원형 극장의 잔해도 볼 수 있다. 거기에 있는 동안 로마 역사박물관도 꼭 방문하는 것이 좋다.

Chester is a Roman town and you can still see many Roman sites there today. The most important of the sites is the City Walls which are the most intact city walls in Britain. You can easily walk around the walls; these were the walls of the original fort. They are about 3km long and surround the original town. They were built between 70 AD and 80 AD. You can also see the remains of a Roman amphitheatre. Make sure you visit the Roman History Museum while you're there.

체스터를 가로지르는 디 강(the River Dee)은 항해와 카누, 보트 여행의 중심지다. 또한, 긴 산책과 소풍을 하기에도 멋진 환경이다. 로마 사람들은 디 강을 체스터 데바(Chester Deva)라고 불렀다. 강은 로마 사람들에게 중요한 무역 경로였고, 데바에는 도시에 필요한 물품을 들여올 수 있는 큰 항구가 있었다. 항구는 이제 더는 그곳에 없다.

The River Dee runs through Chester and it is a centre for sailing, canoeing, and boat trips. It is also a lovely setting for long walks and picnics. The Romans called Chester Deva after the River Dee. The river was a significant trade route for the Romans and Deva had a large harbour to bring in the goods the city needed. The harbour is no longer there.

체스터 궁전은 서기 11세기에 대성당과 함께 건설이 시작되었다. 대성당은 서기 1535년에서야 비로소 완공되었다.

The construction of Chester Castle started in the 11th century AD, at the same time as the cathedral. The cathedral was finally finished in 1535 AD.

체스터는 아마도 차곡차곡 쌓아 올려진 검은색과 흰색의 건물들 때문에 가장 유명하지 않을까 싶다. 이들은 "체스터 로우즈(The Rows)"라고 불린다. 오늘날, 주요 쇼핑센터와 그랜드 호텔인 그로스 버너(The Grosvenor)가 여기에 있다.

Chester is perhaps most famous for its black and white buildings which sit on top of each other. They are called 'The Rows'. Today, these contain the main shopping centre and a grand hotel, The Grosvenor.

도시의 중심은 로마 주요 도로 4개가 교차하는 곳에 크로스(Cross)로 표시되어 있다.

The centre of the city is marked with a Cross, which stands at the point where the 4 main Roman roads meet.

조금은 색다른, 거대한 역사 탐험을 할 곳을 찾는다면, 체스터를 고려해라.

If you want to visit somewhere a little different with a huge amount of history to explore, think of Chester.

아름다운 곳이다.

It's beautiful.

Difficult Words

1- 국경 – Border
2- 시골 도시 – County town
3- 마을 – Town
4- 장벽 – Walls
5- ~정도 – About
6- 지어진 – Built
7- 잔해 – Remains
8- 십자 – Cross
9- 항해 – Sailing
10- 보트 여행 – Boat trips
11- 항구 – Harbour
12- 성 – Castle
13- 완공되다 – Finished
14- 빌딩 – Buildings
15- 체스터 로우즈 – The Rows

이야기 요약 :

체스터는 영국의 북서쪽 지방에 위치한 시골도시이다. 이번 이야기에선, 이 도시의 로마 역사와 현 위치와의 연관성에 대해 설명하고 있다.

Summary of the Story:

Chester is the county town of England located in the north-west of the country. This story describes the Roman history of this city and makes connections to its current locations.

Quiz:

1) 도시 장벽의 길이는 얼마인가?

   a) 10 km

   b) 5 km

   c) 3 km

1) How many kilometers long is The City Wall?

   a) 10 km

   b) 5 km

   c) 3 km

2) 디강(Dee River) 인근에서 찾을 수 있는 것은 :

   a) 상품을 들여오는 큰 항구

   b) 항해, 카누 그리고 보트 여행을 위한 센터

   c) 거대한 성당

2) Near the Dee River, we can currently find:

   a) A large port to bring in the goods.

   b) A center for sailing, canoeing, and boat trips.

   c) A big cathedral.

3) 다음중 틀린 진술은?

   a) 체스터 성의 건설은 성당의 건설과 같은 해에 시작되었다.

   b) 체스터는 화려한 색상의 건물들로 유명하다.

   c) 성당은 서기 1535년에 준공되었다.

3) Which of these statements is false?

   a) The construction of Chester Castle started at the same time as the cathedral.

   b) Chester is famous for its colorful buildings.

   c) The cathedral was finished in 1535 AD.

ANSWERS:

   1) C

   2) B

   3) B

이야기 16: 가족 휴가 – 파트 1
STORY 16: A FAMILY HOLIDAY – PART 1

어느 저녁 사라와 피터는 와인 한 잔을 가지고 앉는다. 헨리는 침대에서 잠들었고 강아지 찰리는 그들의 발 가까이 바닥에서 잠들었다.

Sarah and Peter sit down with a glass of wine one evening. Henry is asleep in bed and Charlie, the dog, is asleep on the floor at their feet.

" 올해 휴가 가고 싶어? " 피터가 사라에게 묻는다. " 그렇다면, 어디에 가고 싶어? "

"Do you want to go on holiday this year," Peter asks Sarah. "And if you do, where do you want to go?"

사라는 잠시 생각한 끝에, " 응, 좀 떠나면 좋겠어. 새 일이 좋긴 하지만 쉴 때가 된 것 같아. " 라고 말한다.

Sarah thinks for a few moments and says, "Yes, it will be nice to get away. My new job is great but I am ready for a break."

" 우리 그럼 어디에 갈까? 좋은 생각 있어? " 피터가 다시 묻는다.

"Where shall we go then? Any ideas?" asks Peter again.

둘이 함께 의견을 나눈다. 그리스, 이탈리아, 포르투갈. 좀 더 멀리 이집트, 튀니지, 터키 아니면 미국도 괜찮고. 그것도 아니면 영국?

They both make some suggestions. Greece, Italy, Portugal. Perhaps further afield to Egypt, Tunisia, Turkey, or even the United States. Or maybe England?

그러자 사라가, " 휴가를 어디로 갈지 결정하기 전에 뭘 할지 먼저 결정할까? 내 말은, 우리가 하고 싶은것뿐만이 아니라 우리 헨리도 생각해야 하고, 걔가 뭘 좋아할지도 생각해야 하잖아. " 라고 한다.

Then Sarah asks, "Can we decide what we want to do on holiday before we decide where to go? I mean, we have to think about Henry and what he will enjoy, not just what we want to do."

피터가 동의하며, " 글쎄, 나한테 달렸다면, 따뜻하고 햇살 좋은 해변에 누워서 수영하러 가고, 맥주 마시고, 집안일은 아무것도 안 해도 되는 곳으로 가겠지. " 그리고는, " 그렇지만 헨리가 좋아하지 않을 거야, 그렇지? 걔는 뭔가 계속 움직이면서 활동적이어야 하니까. 이것 참, 우리가 모두 좋아하고 즐길 수 있는 건 하나도 생각이 안 나네. " 라고 덧붙인다.

Peter agrees saying, "Well, if it were up to me, I would just go and lie on a beach somewhere warm and sunny, go swimming, drink beer, and not have to do any house work." Then he adds, "But Henry wouldn't enjoy that, would he? He needs to be busy and active. Oh dear, I can't think of anything that we will all enjoy and benefit from."

그들은 조용히 앉아 어떻게 하면 헨리를 기쁘게 하면서도 우리가 편할지 생각해 본다.

They each sit in silence and consider what they can do that will make Henry happy, and also make their lives easy.

드디어, 피터가 " 파리 디즈니랜드! 파리 디즈니랜드는 어때? 우리 항상 가야겠다고 말하잖아. 그리고 헨리도 바쁘게 뛰어다니면서 멋진 시간을 보낼 수 있을 거야. 어떻게 생각해? "라고 외친다.

Eventually, Peter shouts out, "Disneyland Paris! What about Disneyland Paris? We always say we should go and I know Henry would be busy and would have a fantastic time. What do you think?"

사라가 피터를 미소지으며 돌아보고, " 그거 진짜 완벽할 거야. 우리 모두 분주하면서도 재밌게 보낼 수 있을 거야. 헨리는 넘치는 에너지를 다 쓸 수 있을 테고, 기억할만한 멋진 경험이 될 거야. 정말 좋은 생각이야. 계획을 세우자! " 라고 말한다.

Sarah turns to Peter smiling and says, "I think that would be perfect. We would all be busy and having fun at the same time. Henry will use up a lot of his energy, and it will be a great experience to remember. What a great suggestion. Let's start planning!"

Difficult Words

1- 와인 – Wine
2- 유리잔 – Glass
3- 잠이 든 – Asleep
4- 발 – Feet
5- 묻다 – Asks
6- 마시다 – Drink
7- 행복한 – Happy
8- 소리지르다 – Shouts
9- 즐겁게 보내다 – Having fun
10- 계획하는 – Planning
11- 삶 – Life
12- 고려하다 – Consider
13- 우리는 즐길 것이다 – We will enjoy
14- 얼마 안 되는 시간 – Few moments
15- 휴식 시간 – Break

이야기 요약 :

사라와 남편 피터는 다음 휴가를 계획중이다. 모두가 다른 활동을 원할 때, 또 아들 헨리가 좋아할 만한 것을 생각하다보면 고려해야 할 것이 한 둘이 아니다. 과연 이번 해 휴가는 어디로 정해질 것인가?

Summary of the Story:

Sarah and her husband Peter are thinking about their next vacation. There is a lot to consider when deciding where to go, as everyone wants to do different activities and they also have to think about what their son Henry would like to do. What will they choose this year for the holidays?

Quiz:

1) 피터가 휴가때 하고 싶은 것은?
  a) 이집트 방문
  b) 디즈니랜드 방문
  c) 해변에 누워있고, 수영을 하고, 맥주를 마시는 일

1) What would Peter like to do for the holidays?
  a) He would like to go in Egypt.
  b) He would like to go at Disneyland.
  c) He would like to lie on a beach, go swimming and drink beer.

2) 파리 디즈니랜드가 왜 좋은 아이디어인듯 할까?
  a) 모두가 함께 즐거운 시간을 보낼 수 있기 때문에
  b) 헨리가 가보길 너무나 원해서
  c) 휴가기간 동안 헨리를 돌볼 시간이 없어서

2) Why Disneyland Paris seams a perfect idea?
  a) Because they would all be busy and having fun at the same time.
  b) Because Henry dreams to go there.
  c) Because they won't have to take care of Henry during the Holidays.

3) 사라와 피터로부터 제안되지 않은 나라는?
  a) 포르투갈
  b) 캐나다
  c) 터키

3) Which country is not proposed by Sarah and Peter?
  a) Portugal
  b) Canada
  c) Turkey

ANSWERS:
  1) C
  2) A
  3) B

이야기 17: 가족 휴가 – 파트 2
STORY 17: A FAMILY HOLIDAY – PART 2

결정은 내려졌다. 그들은 파리 디즈니랜드로 휴가를 떠날 것이다. 계획을 시작할 시간이다.

The decision is made. They're going to Disneyland Paris for their holiday. It's time to start planning.

사라와 피터는 파리 디즈니랜드를 알아보기 위해 온라인에 접속한다. 어떻게 가는지부터 시작한다.

Sarah and Peter go online to start researching Disneyland Paris. They start with how to get there.

여러 가지 방법이 있는 듯 보인다. 비행 후 버스를 타거나 기차를 갈아타는 방법이 있고, 아니면 직접 운전해 갈 수도 있다. 운전하는 것이 좋아서 그러기로 한다. 주차할 공간이 많아서 문제가 되지 않을 것이다.

It seems they have a number of options. They can either fly and then take a bus, travel by train with some changes, or drive there themselves. They like the idea of driving so they decide that is what they will do. There is plenty of parking so that won't be a problem.

그들은 숙소를 알아보기 시작하고 헨리가 즐길 수 있는 디즈니랜드 호텔 중 한 곳에서 지내기로 한다. 찾아보니 호텔들이 모두 서로 다르고 크기도 어마어마하다는 것을 알게 된다. 리조트 호텔 중 하나에 머무르면 매일 놀이공원에 걸어갈 수도 있고 헨리가 더는 걸을 수 없는 상황에는 버스를 타고 돌아올 수도 있다.

They then start to look at accommodation and decide it will be more fun for Henry if they stay in one of the Disneyland Hotels. When they start looking at them, they realise that they are all very different, and that they're huge. Staying in one of the resort hotels means that they can walk into the park each day but, if necessary, take a bus back in the evening when Henry's legs won't work anymore.

그들은 서로 다른 호텔과 각양각색의 테마를 살펴본다. 뉴포트 만 클럽이 좋아 보이지만 카우보이와 인디언을 좋아하는 헨리는 샤이엔 호텔을 더 좋아할 것 같다. 그래서, 샤이엔 호텔로 정한다. 그들은 날짜와 비용, 예약 가능한지를 살펴본다.

They look at the different hotels and their different themes. They like the look of the Newport Bay Club but think that Henry will prefer the Hotel Cheyenne as he loves cowboys and Indians. So, the Hotel Cheyenne it is. They look at dates, costs, and availability.

그리고는 얼마 동안 가 있을지 생각해본다. 방문하여 즐길 수 있는 놀이공원의 두 구역과 함께, 다른 할 것이 있는지 세부사항을 살펴보기 시작한다. 놀이기구나 쇼, 만날 수 있는 캐릭터, 충분히 즐길 수 있는 분위기도. 3박 4일이면 놀이공원에서 즐기기에 충분할 것이라고 결정한다.

They then start to think about how long they will go for. With the 2 sides of the park to visit and enjoy, they start to look in detail at what exactly there is to do. Rides, shows, characters to meet, and the atmosphere to soak up. They decide 3 nights with 4 days in the park will be just right.

예약하려던 찰나 찰리를 떠올린다. 떠나 있는 동안 찰리는 어떻게 해야 할까? 찰리를 돌봐줄 만큼 강아지를 좋아하는 사람도 없고, 근처 개 사육장도 모른다.

They are about to make a booking when they stop and realise that they have Charlie to think about. What will they do with Charlie while they are away? They don't know anybody who likes dogs enough to look after him for them, and they don't know any kennels nearby.

그러다 파리 디즈니랜드를 방문하는 사람들을 위한 애완동물 센터가 있다는 것을 알아차린다. 완벽한 해결책 - 찰리도 휴가를 보낸다!

Then they notice that Disneyland Paris has a pet centre for the pets of people visiting the park. Perfect solution – Charlie will have a holiday too!

Difficult Words

1- 시작하다 – To start
2- 어마어마한 (크기) – Huge
3- 걷다 – To walk
4- 저녁 – The evening
5- 다리 – Legs
6- 예약 가능성 – Availability
7- 구역 – Sides
8- 놀이기구 – Rides
9- 쇼, 공연 – Shows
10- 캐릭터 – Characters
11- 분위기 – Atmosphere
12- 흠뻑 빠져들다 – To soak up
13- 개 사육장 – Kennels
14- 근처 – Nearby
15- 반려동물 – Pets

이야기 요약 :

결정되었다. 사라와 피터 가족은 휴가로 파리의 디즈니랜드에 간다. 이제 방문 계획을 세워야 한다.

Summary of the Story :

The decision is made. Sarah and Peter's family will go to Disneyland Paris for their vacation. Now they have to plan their visit.

Quiz:

1) 파크 근처 호텔에 묶었을때의 장점은?
   a) 매일 걸어서 파크에 가고 버스를 타고 돌아올 수 있다.
   b) 이미 공원 내에 있기 때문에 시간을 절약할 수 있다.
   c) 공원 밖 호텔보다 저렴하여 비용을 절약할 수 있다.

1) What is the main advantage of staying in one of the resort hotel of the park?
   a) They can walk into the park each day and come back at their hotel by bus.
   b) They will save time because they are already on the site.
   c) They will save money because hotels of the site are cheaper than outside of the park.

2) 얼마나 묶을 것인가?
   a) 4박 3일
   b) 2박 3일
   c) 3박 4일

2) How long is their stay?
   a) 4 nights and 3 days
   b) 2 nights and 3 days
   c) 3 nights and 4 days

3) 찰리는 누구인가?
   a) 헨리의 친구
   b) 가족이 키우는 개
   c) 가족이 키우는 고양이

3) Who is Charlie?
   a) The friend of Henry
   b) The family's dog
   c) The family's cat

ANSWERS:
   1) A
   2) C
   3) B

이야기 18: 가족 휴가 - 파트 3
STORY 18: A FAMILY HOLIDAY - PART 3

출발 후 몇 시간의 운전 끝에, 고속도로를 벗어나 파리 디즈니랜드에 있는 호텔로 들어선다. 헨리는 매우 들떴다! 찰리는 자기도 휴가를 보내는 줄은 모르지만 어쨌든 들떴다.

They set off and after several hours of travelling, they pull off the autoroute and make their way to their hotel at Disneyland Paris. Henry is so excited! Charlie is not aware that he is having a holiday too, but he is excited anyway.

사라, 피터 그리고 헨리가 샤이엔 호텔에 체크인하는 동안 찰리는 차 안에 남겨둔다. 방은 근사하고 헨리는 2층 침대에서 잔다고 들떠 한다. 그는 위에서 잘지 침대 아래에서 잘지 결정을 못 한다. 정말 힘든 결정이 아닐 수 없다!

Sarah, Peter and Henry book in to the Hotel Cheyenne and leave Charlie in the car for a while. The room is amazing and Henry is very excited to be sleeping in a bunk bed. He can't decide whether to sleep on the top or the bottom bunk. What a decision!

몇 분 후에, 차로 돌아가 찰리를 데리고 오기로 한다.

After a few minutes, they decide to go back to the car and collect Charlie.

" 우리 지금 놀이공원으로 가서 찰리를 호텔에 맡길까? " 피터가 헨리에게 제안한다. 그들은 파크에 가서 방문자 주차장에 있는 동물 센터를 찾는다. 찰리를 맡기고 나서 찰리도 자기 호텔에서 행복하리라 생각하며 놀이공원으로 돌아온다.

"Shall we head to the park now and check Charlie in to his hotel?" Peter suggests to Henry. They go to the park and find the animal centre which is in the visitor parking area. They check Charlie in and head off towards the park, knowing that he will be happy in his hotel too.

그들은 주변에 울려 퍼지는 행복한 디즈니 음악을 들으며 경쾌하게 걷는다. 정문에 도착해 가방 검색대를 지난다.

They can hear the happy Disney music all around them and walk with a spring in their step. They arrive at the main entrance and go through the bag security checks.

그리고는 결정을 해야 한다: 오리지널 디즈니랜드로 가서 전통적인 디즈니 놀이기구를 탈지 아니면 월트 디즈니 스튜디오로 갈지. 정말 어려운 선택이 아닐 수 없다!

Then they have to make a decision: whether to go into the main park - the original Disney Park - and do the traditional Disney rides, or whether to go in to Walt Disney Studios. What a choice!

그래서, 사라가 헨리에게, " 어디서부터 시작할까, 헨리야? " 하고 묻는다.

So, Sarah asks Henry, "Where shall we start, Henry?"

헨리에게는 쉬운 선택이다. " 디즈니랜드로 가서 캐릭터 좀 찾아봐요! "

For Henry, it's an easy decision. "Let's go into the Disney Park and look for some characters."

그래서 거기로 가기로 한다.

So that's where they go.

곧바로, 중심 거리의 시작에 있는 철도역 근처에서 웃는 사람들에 둘러싸인 플루토를 발견한다. 그를 지나쳐서 가던 길을 계속 가는데 갑자기, 미키 마우스와 미니 마우스가 그들을 향해 걸어오는 것을 본다. 이번에는 사람들도 없어서 헨리가 그들에게 인사하러 달려간다.

Straightaway, they see Pluto near the railway station at the start of Main Street, and he is surrounded by smiling people. They decide to carry on past him and suddenly see, walking towards them, Mickey and Minnie Mouse. This time, there is no crowd of people and Henry runs towards them to say hello.

미키 마우스와 미니 마우스가 웃으며 손을 흔들고는 헨리에게 ' 하이파이브 ' 를 한다. 그리고 피터가 셋을 함께 사진으로 담는다. 헨리는 그들에게 찰리에 대한 모든 것과 그들이 지내고 있는 호텔에 관해 이야기하고 미키 마우스와 미니 마우스는 웃으며 잘 들어준다.

Mickey and Minnie smile and wave and 'high five' Henry. And Peter takes a photograph of the three of them together. Henry tells them all about Charlie and the hotel they're staying at and Mickey and Minnie listen with interest, smiling.

헨리는 너무 들떠서 이야기를 멈추지 않는다.

Henry is so excited and doesn't stop talking.

Difficult Words

1- 그들은 출발하였다. – They set off
2- 놀라운 – Amazing
3- 벙크 침대 – Bunk bed
4- 데리고 오다 – To collect
5- (호텔) 체크인 하다 – They check in
6- 출발하다 – Head off
7- 듣다 – To hear
8- 정문 – Main entrance
9- 가방들 – Bags
10- 웃으며 – Smiling
11- 뛰다 – Runs
12- 흥미 – Interest
13- 둘러싸인 – Surrounded
14- 알고있는 – Knowing
15- 방 – Room

이야기 요약 :

사라, 피터 그리고 헨리가 마침내 휴가를 위해 파리의 디즈이랜드에 도착하며 디데이가 되었다.

Summary of the Story :

It's finally D-Day for Sarah, Peter and Henry since they finally arrived at Disneyland Paris for the holidays. Henry is so excited by this new adventure.

Quiz:

1) 찰리를 애견 센터에 남겨둘때 해터와 헨리의 기분은 어땠나?

   a) 기뻤다. 찰리가 호텔에서 행복하게 지낼 거란 걸 알기 때문에

   b) 걱정하였다. 찰리가 그들 없이 호텔에서 지내본 적이 없기 때문에

   c) 신이났다. 찰리의 첫 번째 호텔 경험이기 때문에

1) How do Peter and Henry feel when they leave Charlie at the animal center?

   a) Happy, because they know that Charlie will be happy in his hotel too.

   b) Anxious, because Charlie never been in a hotel without them.

   c) Excited, because it will be Charlie's first experience in a hotel.

2) 그들이 가장 먼저 하기로 한 것은?

   a) 원조 디즈니 파크에 가는 것

   b) 월트 디즈니 스튜디오에 가는 것.

   c) 전통 디즈니 놀이기구를 타는 것

2) What do they choose to do first?

   a) To go the Original Disney Park.

   b) To go in the Walt Disney Studio.

   c) To do the traditional Disney rides.

3) 그들이 가장 처음 본 캐릭터는?

   a) 미니마우스

   b) 미키마우스

   c) 플루토

3) Who is the first character that they see?

   a) Minnie Mouse

   b) Mickey Mouse

   c) Pluto

ANSWERS:

   1) A

   2) A

   3) C

이야기 19: 가족 휴가 – 파트 4
STORY 19: A FAMILY HOLIDAY – PART 4

미키 마우스와 미니 마우스를 만난 후에, 헨리는 이다음에 무엇을 할지 결정을 못 해 피터가 놀이공원 일정을 골라 건넨다.

After his adventure with Mickey and Minnie Mouse, Henry can't decide what he wants to do next, so Peter picks up a plan of the park and hands it to him.

" 앉아서 거기에서 뭘 할지 한번 보자. 그러고 나서 결정하면 돼. " 사라가 말한다.

"Let's sit down and see exactly what there is to do. Then we can decide," says Sarah.

헨리는 배가 고프다며 다른 것을 하기 전에 먼저 먹을 수 있을지 묻는다. 좋은 생각이다.

Henry says he's rather hungry so asks if they can eat before they do anything else. Good idea.

일정표를 이용해서, 다양한 식당을 보는데 헨리가 감자튀김을 먹고 싶다며 강하게 말한다. 감자튀김과 같이 먹을 음식은 상관없지만, 어쨌든 감자튀김은 먹어야 한다. 그들은, 헨리는 햄버거와 감자튀김을, 사라와 피터는 닭고기와 샐러드를 먹을 수 있는 식당을 선택한다.

Using the plan, they look at the different restaurants and Henry declares that he wants chips. He doesn't mind what he has with his chips, but he wants chips. They select a restaurant where Henry can have a burger with chips and Sarah and Peter can have chicken and salad.

음식을 주문하고 앉아서 먹으며 놀이공원 일정표를 살펴본다. 음식은 고급 프랑스 요리는 아니지만 괜찮다. 그들은 붐비는 놀이기구를 타기 위해 줄을 서야 한다는 것을 알지만, 재밌는 놀이기구들이 가까이에 있다는 것을 알고는 피터 팬을 먼저 타기로 한다. 다 먹은 후, 피터 팬 놀이기구로 걸어가 차례를 기다린다.

When they have bought their food, they sit down and eat, and look at the park plan. The food isn't French haute cuisine but it's perfectly fine. They know they will have to queue for the rides as it is so busy, but they realise that they are near to some good rides and so agree to try Peter Pan first. When they finish eating, they walk over to the Peter Pan ride and wait for their turn.

놀이기구에 탈 차례가 되어 자리에 앉았을 때, 헨리는 아주 많이 들떴지만 금방 잠이 들어 사라에게 기댄 채 놀이기구 나머지 부분을 모두 놓친다. 사라와 피터는 내일 충분한 힘을 내기 위해 호텔로 돌아가 잠을 잘 시간이라 결정한다.

많이 걷고 신나는 일도 많은 긴 하루가 될 것이기 때문에 모두 푹 쉬어야 한다고 느낀다.

When they join the ride and take their seat, Henry is very excited but within just a few seconds, he falls asleep, leaning against Sarah, and misses the rest of the ride. Sarah and Peter decide it's time to go back to the hotel and get some sleep so that they have enough energy for the next day. It will be a long day with lots of walking and lots of excitement, so they agree that they all need a good night's sleep.

피터가 헨리를 버스 정류장으로 옮기고 호텔로 돌아가는 버스를 탄다. 헨리를 깨우지 않고 침대에 눕힌 후 찬찬히 살펴보려 앉는다. 놀이공원 일정표를 보고 내일은 어디에서부터 시작할지 결정하려고 하지만, 그러기엔 너무 피곤하다는 걸 깨닫고 잠자리에 든다.

Peter carries Henry to the bus stop, then they catch the bus back to their hotel. They put Henry to bed without him waking up and sit down themselves to take it all in. They look at the plan of the parks to try to decide where to start tomorrow, but then agree they are too tired, and head to bed themselves.

Difficult Words

1- 배고픈 – Hungry
2- 그는 개의치 않다 – He doesn't mind
3- 감자튀김 – Chips
4- 닭고기 – Chicken
5- 고급 요리 – Haute cuisine
6- 정말 괜찮다 – Perfectly fine
7- 시도하다 – To try
8- 배우는 – Leaning
9- ~에 기대어 – Against
10- 나르다 – Carries
11- 내일 – Tomorrow
12- 깨닫다 – Realise
13- 놓치다 – Misses
14- 그 밖에 다른 것 – Anything else
15- 차례 – Turn

줄거리 :

여전히 사라와 피터 가족의 디즈니랜드 파크 방문의 첫째 날이다. 미키, 미니마우스와 대화 후, 가족은 남은 하루 동안 어떤 활동을 할 것인지를 정해야 했다.

Summary of the Story :

It's still the first day at Disneyland Paris for the family of Sarah and Peter. After talking with Mickey and Minnie Mouse, the family must make decisions about what activities to do during the rest of the day.

Quiz:

1) 파리 디즈니 랜드에서 한 첫 번째 식사는?
  a) 고급요리는 아니었지만 충분히 괜찮은 음식
  b) 고급요리이고 엄청난 음식
  c) 고급요리가 아니고 좋지 못한 음식

1) How is their first meal at Disneyland Paris?
   a) The food isn't haute cuisine, but it's good enough.
   b) The food is haute cuisine and excellent.
   c) The food isn't haute cuisine and not very good.

2) 다음날은 하기로 계획한 것은?
  a) 피터 팬 놀이기구 타기
  b) 호텔 근처 놀이기구 타기
  c) 너무 피곤해서 계획을 세우지 못함

2) What do they decide to do to start their next day?
   a) They will go to Peter Pan ride.
   b) They will start by the rides near the hotel.
   c) They don't decide, because they are too tired.

3) 이맘때에 이곳엔 :
  a) 많은 사람들이 있다
  b) 사람들이 별로 없다
  c) 평소처럼 많은 사람들이 있다

3) In this time of the year, there is:
   a) A lot of people
   b) Not many people
   c) As many people as usual

ANSWERS:
   1) A
   2) C
   3) B

이야기 20: 가족 휴가 – 파트 5
STORY 20: A FAMILY HOLIDAY – PART 5

디즈니랜드로의 여행 두 번째 날.
Day two of the trip to Disneyland.

헨리는 아주 피곤하지만 매우 들뜬 기분으로 일어난다. 그는 빨리 아침 식사를 하고 놀이공원으로 가고 싶어 한다. 아침 식사로 초콜릿 시리얼을 먹고 빵과 잼, 마실 것으로는 오렌지 주스와 뜨거운 코코아를 먹는다.
Henry wakes up feeling very tired but very excited. He's keen to go to breakfast early and then into the park. For breakfast he chooses chocolate cereal followed by bread and jam, with orange juice and a hot chocolate to drink.

그들은 놀이동산으로 다시 걸어가며 오늘은 매우 덥다고 이야기한다. 보안 검색대를 다시 지난 후, 봐야 할 것은 모두 볼 수 있는 기차를 타고 놀이동산을 돌아보기로 한다. 헨리는 다양한 놀이기구를 보는 것에 들떠서 타고 싶은 놀이기구 목록을 만들기 시작한다.
They walk to the park again and comment that it is very hot today. They go through security again, and decide to take the train around the park so that they can see everything there is to see. Henry is excited to see so many different rides and starts to make a list of the rides he wants to go to.

음료를 마시기 전에 놀이기구를 두 개 더 탄다. 사라가 두통이 있고 메스껍다며 몸이 좋지 않고 뭔가 먹어야겠다고 한다. 줄에 서서 기다려야 하는데 사라가 공황 상태에 빠지며 의식을 잃고는 머리를 바닥에 부딪힌다. 헨리가 울기 시작하고 피터는 사라 옆 바닥에서 그녀에게 말을 걸고 상태를 확인한다. 그는 그녀의 머리에 난 상처를 발견한다.
They do two more rides before deciding to stop for a drink. Sarah says she is feeling unwell – she has a headache and feels nauseous - and needs something to eat as well. They have to queue and Sarah starts to panic, faints, and hits her head on the floor. Henry starts to cry and Peter gets on to the floor next to Sarah to talk to her and check on her. He sees she has a cut on her head.

세 명의 디즈니랜드 직원이 급히 도우러 오며 레모네이드와 코카콜라 음료를 두 개 가져와 사라의 혈당 수치를 위해 마시라고 권한다.
Three Disneyland staff rush over to help, and bring two drinks, lemonade and Coca-Cola, which they encourage Sarah to drink to help her blood sugar levels.

그녀가 레모네이드를 마시고 코카콜라를 헨리에게 건네자 헨리는 울음을 멈춘다.
She drinks the lemonade and gives the Coca-Cola to Henry, and he stops crying.

한 남자가 휠체어를 가지고 나타났고 사라가 괜찮은지 확인하기 위해 의료센터로 수송한다. 상처에서 계속 피가 났기 때문에 그들은 사라에게 엑스레이 검사를 하고 상처를 꿰맬 수 있도록 가장 가까운 병원을 알아봐 주고, 피터와 헨리도 그녀와 함께 간다.

A man appears with a wheelchair and Sarah is taken to the medical centre to be checked over. The cut keeps bleeding so they arrange for Sarah to go to the nearest hospital for an X-Ray and stitches, and Peter and Henry go with her.

그녀는 병원에서 바로 즉시 의사를 만나고, 왜 의식을 잃었는지 확인하기 위해 많은 검사를 해야 한다. 그들은 그녀가 매우 덥고 피곤하다는 것 이외의 다른 이유는 찾지 못한다. 그들은 그녀의 머리를 꿰맨 후 그들 모두 다시 휴가를 계속하기 위해 디즈니랜드로 돌아간다.

She sees a doctor at the hospital very quickly and has lots of tests to check why she fainted. They do not find a reason, other than her being very hot and very tired. They stitch her head and then they all go back to Disneyland to continue their holiday.

디즈니랜드 직원은 매우 다정하게 사라를 걱정하며 그들이 놀이동산에 도착했을 때 무료 식사를 제공한다. 그들은 꽤 배가 고팠기 때문에 감사히 받아들인다.

The Disneyland staff is very caring and worried about Sarah and offer them a free meal when they are back in the park. They accept gratefully as they are rather hungry.

Difficult Words

1- 더운 – Hot
2- 공황상태에 빠진 – Panic
3- 두통 – Headache
4- 메스꺼움 – Nauseous
5- 기절하다 – Faints
6- 부딪히다 – Hits
7- 울다 – To cry
8- 이야기 하다 – To talk
9- 상처 – Cut
10- 직원 – Staff
11- 황급히 달려가다 – Rush over
12- 가지고 오다 – Bring
13- 피 – Blood
14- 휠체어 – Wheelchair
15- 바늘땀 – Stitches

이야기 요약 :

파리 디즈니랜드에서의 두번째 날이다. 날은 따뜻하고 화창하였으며, 헨리는 하루를 시작하기에 앞서 매우 흥분되어 있었다. 그러나 무언가 계획한 대로 되지 않는데…

Summary of the Story :

This is the second day at Disneyland Paris, the weather is warm and beautiful, and Henry is very excited to start his day. However, something is not going as planned.

Quiz:

1) 사라의 상처를 가장 먼저 발견한 사람은?
   a) 헨리
   b) 의사
   c) 피터

1) Who first notices the cut on Sarah's head?
   a) Henry
   b) The doctor
   c) Peter

2) 사라가 기절한 것을 보고 헨리가 어떻게 반응하였는가?
   a) 울음을 터뜨렸다.
   b) 공황상태에 빠졌다.
   c) 차분히 도움을 요청했다.

2) How does Henry react when Sarah passes out?
   a) He cries
   b) He panics
   c) He stays calm and asks for help.

3) 사라의 상태를 낫게 하기 위해 직원이 무엇을 가져다주었나?
   a) 초콜렛
   b) 에너지 드링크
   c) 레모네이드와 코카콜라

3) What do the employees bring to Sarah to make her feel better?
   a) Chocolate
   b) An energy drinks
   c) A lemonade and a Coca Cola

ANSWERS:
   1) C
   2) A
   3) C

이야기 21: 집으로 돌아가기
STORY 21: GETTING HOME

피터, 사라, 헨리는 가방을 싸고 샤이엔 호텔을 체크아웃한 후 찰리를 데리러 간다. 그들은 환상적이고 파란만장했던 파리 디즈니랜드 여행을 끝낸 후 차로 걸어가 집으로 향한다.

Peter, Sarah and Henry pack their bags, check out of the Hotel Cheyenne, then go and collect Charlie. They walk back to their car and begin to head for home after their fantastic and eventful trip to Disneyland Paris.

그들은 집으로 가는 가장 짧은 경로가 어디인지 잘 모른다. 파리를 운전해 다니며 집으로 가는 길을 찾기 위해 위성 내비게이션(내비)을 이용해야 할 것 같다. 피터가 주소를 입력하고 방향 안내를 기다린다.

They aren't sure which way to go for the shortest journey home. They need to use satellite navigation (Sat Nav) to help them drive around Paris and to find the right way home. Peter sets the co-ordinates for their address and they wait for their directions.

내비는 짧은 시간에 최적의 경로를 계산한다.

Sat Nav spends a little time working out the best route.

그리고는 내비가 안내한다:

Then Sat Nav says:

- 표시된 경로에 진입하시면 안내가 시작됩니다.
- The guidance will start when you join the highlighted route.
- 중앙 도로에 도착하시면 로터리에서 세 번째 출구로 나오세요.
- When you reach the main road, enter the roundabout and take the third exit.
- 고속도로에서 10km로 계속 직진하세요.
- Continue straight on the motorway for 10 kms.
- 500 미터 앞 다음 교차로에서 계속 우측통행하세요.
- In 500 metres, at the next junction, keep right.
- 150 미터 앞에서 계속 오른쪽 차선을 유지하여 고속도로에 진입하세요.
- After 150 metres, keep right and join the motorway.
- 우측통행하세요.
- Keep right.
- 5km 계속 직진하세요.
- Continue straight for 5 kms.

- 회전교차로에 들어 두 번째 출구로 나오세요.
- Join the roundabout and take the second exit.
- 1km 앞에서 좌측통행하세요.
- In 1km, keep left.
- 고속도로에 진입하세요.
- Join the motorway.
- 100km 동안 고속도로에 머무르세요.
- Stay on the motorway for 100 kms.
- 요금소에 진입합니다. 표를 준비하고 천천히 서행하세요.
- You are approaching a toll booth. Slow down and have your ticket ready.
- 요금소를 지나 계속 좌측통행하세요.
- After the toll, keep left.
- 계속 좌측통행하세요.
- Keep left.
- 102km 동안 계속 직진하세요.
- Continue straight for 102 kms.
- 800m 앞에서 출구로 나가세요.
- In 800 metres, take the exit.
- 고속도로를 나가 계속 좌측통행하세요.
- As you leave the motorway, keep left.
- 다음 출구에서, 우측통행 후 2km 동안 길을 따라가세요.
- At the next exit, keep right and follow the road for 2 kms.
- 목적지에 도착했습니다.
- You have reached your destination.

채널 터널에 가까워지자 그들은 지나갈 요금소를 선택한다.
As they approach the Channel Tunnel, they select a toll booth to approach.

사라와 피터는 자동 요금소를 예약하고 선택했다. 그들은 일찍 도착해서 터널을 통해 일찍 기차를 탈 수 있다는 사실을 확인하고 만족한다.
Sarah and Peter have pre-booked and select the automated booth. They have arrived early and are pleased to see that they can take an earlier train through the Tunnel.

터미널에서 코드가 불리기를 기다리는 동안 점심으로 먹을 샌드위치를 산다.
They wait in the terminal for their letter code to be announced and buy some sandwiches for lunch while they are waiting.

15분 후에, 그들의 코드가 불리고 집으로 돌아가는 기차로 운전해 올라가기 위해 차로 돌아간다.

After 15 minutes, their letter code is called and they walk back to their car to drive to the train and the return home.

Difficult Words

1- 많은 일들이 있었던 – Eventful
2- 길 – Way
3- 사용하다 – To use
4- 찾다 – To find
5- 좌표를 설정하다 – Co-ordinates
6- 표시된 – Highlighted
7- 회전교차로 – Roundabout
8- 출구 – Exit
9- 서행하다 – Slow down
10- 좌측 – Left
11- 우측 – Right
12- 두 번째 – Second
13- 직진 – Straight
14- 고속도로 – Motorway
15- 머무르다 – Stay

이야기 요약 :

피터, 사라 그리고 헨리는 파리 디즈니랜드에서의 환상적인 휴일을 보내고 이제 집으로 돌아갈 준비를 하고 있다. 그들은 돌아가는 길을 준비하고 목적지까지 가기 위해서 GPS를 신중하게 듣고 있다.

Summary of the Story :

Peter, Sarah and Henry have finished their fantastic vacation at Disneyland Paris and are now ready to head home. They therefore prepare for the return trip and listen carefully to the GPS to find their way back.

Quiz:

1) 회전 교차로와 요금소까지의 거리는 몇 킬로미터인가?
   a) 10 km
   b) 100 km
   c) 102 km

1) There are how many kilometers between the roundabout and the toll booth?
   a) 10 km
   b) 100 km
   c) 102 km

2) 사라와 피터가 해협 터널에 :
   a) 늦게 도착하였다
   b) 일찍 도착하였다
   c) 기차에 탑승하기 딱 알맞은 시간에 도착하였다

2) Sarah and Peter arrive at the Channel Tunnel
   a) Late
   b) In advance
   c) Just in time for their train

3) 그들의 코드 번호가 불려지기를 기다리는 동안 그들이 구매한 것은?
   a) 시간 때우기용 게임
   b) 음료
   c) 샌드위치

3) What are they buying while waiting for their letter code to be announced?
   a) Games to pass the time
   b) Drinks
   c) Sandwiches

ANSWERS:
   1) B
   2) B
   3) C

이야기 22: 쇼핑과 점심 나들이 (1)
STORY 22: OUT SHOPPING AND FOR LUNCH (1)

사라는 파리 디즈니랜드에서의 일 후에 좀 괜찮아졌다.
Sarah is feeling better after her problem at Disneyland Paris.

직장으로 돌아가기 전에, 친구 나탈리와 만나 점심을 먹기로 계획한다.
Before she goes back to work, she arranges to meet a friend – Natalie - for lunch.

그들은 금요일에 마을에서 만나 점심을 먹기 전에 쇼핑하러 간다.
They meet in town on Friday and go shopping before having lunch.

사라는 새 직장에서 입을 새 옷이 필요하다고 생각한다: 정장, 스마트 셔츠, 원피스 그리고 새 신발도 꼭 필요하다.
*참고: 스마트셔츠 (smart shirt) 는 생체신호를 측정하는 특수 기능을 지닌 셔츠이다.
Sarah decides she needs some new clothes for work: a suit, a smart shirt, a dress, and definitely some new shoes.

그들은 대형 백화점에 들어가 숙녀복 매장에서 맞을만한 옷을 보기 시작한다.
They go first into a large department store and start looking for suitable clothes in the ladies' clothes departments.

사라가 천천히 둘러보지만 좋아할 만한 것은 보이지 않는다. 나탈리가 제안하지만 사라는 여전히 흥미가 없다. 그러다, 그녀는 좋아하는 파란색 원피스를 발견하고 입어 본다. 그녀는 너무 크다고 하며 좀 더 작은 사이즈를 달라고 한다. 또한, 초록색으로 있는지 물어본다. 초록은 그녀가 제일 좋아하는 색이다. 초록색은 없고 파란색만 있다.
Sarah walks around slowly but sees nothing she likes. Natalie makes some suggestions but still Sarah is not interested. Suddenly, she sees a blue dress that she likes, and tries it on. She says it is too big and she asks for a smaller size. She also asks if it is available in green. Green is her favourite colour. It is not available in green, only in blue.

그녀는 좀 더 작은 사이즈를 입어보지만, 너무 작아서 계속 둘러본다.
She tries the smaller size and it feels too small so she keeps looking.

또 다른 남색 원피스를 보고 입어 본다. 이번에는 너무 작아서, 재고가 있는 좀 더 큰 사이즈를 달라고 해 입어본다. 몸에 딱 맞고 나탈리도 보기 좋다고 해서, 사라는 구매하기로 한다. 나탈리는 아까 보았던 파란 원피스를 입어보고 딱 맞아서 사기로 한다.

She sees another dress in navy blue and tries it on. This time it is too small, so she asks for a larger size, which is available, then tries that on. It fits perfectly and Natalie says it looks great, so Sarah decides to buy it. Natalie decides to try on the blue dress from earlier and it fits her perfectly, so she decides to buy that for herself.

사라와 나탈리는 적절한 정장을 찾기 위해 다른 매장을 여러 군데 들린다. 사라는 무슨 색을 사야 할지 결정을 하지 못한다. 지적인 느낌이 들면서도 여러 종류의 상의나 셔츠와 함께 입을 수 있는 것을 원한다. 나탈리는 회색 정장을 찾아보라고 권하며 회색은 다양하게 활용할 수 있고 어느 색과도 잘 어울린다고 말한다.

Sarah and Natalie go to a number of different departments to look for a suitable suit. Sarah can't decide what colour she wants. She wants to feel smart but wants to wear the suit with a number of different tops or shirts. Natalie suggests she look for a grey suit, saying grey is very versatile and goes with any colour.

사라는 그녀가 좋아하는 회색 치마를 바로 발견하고 치마와 함께 나온 맞는 사이즈의 재킷을 찾는다. 가게 점원은 치마와 세트로 나온 재킷은 가게에 없다고 말하며 다른 치마를 권하지만, 사라는 회색 치마 만큼 마음에 들지는 않는다. 사라는 실망하여 나탈리에게, "점심 먹을 준비 아직 안 됐어? 나 배고파!" 라고 묻는다.

Sarah is disappointed and asks Natalie, "Are you ready for lunch yet? I'm starving!"

나탈리도 점심을 먹으러 가고 싶어 해서 그들은 어디로 갈지 이야기하기 시작한다.

Natalie is happy to go for lunch and they start to talk about where to go.

Difficult Words

1- 금요일 – Friday
2- 옷 – Clothes
3- 스마트 셔츠 – A smart shirt
4- 원피스 – A dress
5- 신발 – Shoes
6- 백화점 – Large department store
7- 사이즈, 치수 – Size
8- 더 작은 – Smaller
9- 재고가 있는 – Available
10- 다양하게 활용 가능한 – Versatile
11- 셔츠 – Skirt
12- 재킷 – Jacket
13- 실망한 – Disappointed
14- 준비된 – Ready
15- 녹색 – Green

이야기 요약 :

사라가 휴가를 보내고 돌아왔다. 사라는 회사로 복귀하기 전 나탈리와 함께 쇼핑데이를 보내며 새롭게 사무실에서 입을 옷을 구매하기로 하였다.

Summary of the Story :

Sarah is back from vacation, but before returning to work, she sees her friend Nathalie and decides to do a shopping day with her to buy new work clothes.

Quiz:

1) 점심시간에 사라가 산 것은?
   a) 회색 스커트와 파란 원피스
   b) 회색 정장과 회색 스커트
   c) 파란 원피스

1) At lunch time Sarah bought :
   a) A grey skirt and a blue dress
   b) A grey suit and grey skirt
   c) A blue dress

2) 점심을 먹으러 가기 전 사라가 느낀 감정은 ?
   a) 구매한 것에 행복해함
   b) 그녀가 좋아하는 셔츠에 어울리는 재킷을 찾지 못해 실망함
   c) 그녀가 원하는 어떤것도 찾지 못해 화가 났음

2) How does Sarah feel before going for lunch?
   a) Really happy with her purchases.
   b) Disappointed for not having found a jacket matching a skirt that she likes.
   c) Angry that she couldn't find everything she wanted.

3) 왜 사라는 좋아하는 정장 색을 결정하지 못하였는가 ?
   a) 그녀는 스마트해 보이길 원했지만, 여러 다른 색의 상의와 어울리게 입어야 했기 때문에
   b) 어떤 색이 자신과 어울리는지 잘 몰라서
   c) 신발색이 아직 결정되지 않아서

3) Why does Sarah can't decide on the color of the suit she would like?
   a) Because she wants to feel smart but wants to wear the suit with a number of different tops or shirts.
   b) Because she doesn't know what color suits her
   c) Because she doesn't know yet the color her shoes will be.

ANSWERS:

1) C
2) B
3) A

이야기 23: 쇼핑과 점심 나들이(2)
STORY 23: OUT SHOPPING AND FOR LUNCH (2)

사라와 나탈리는 점심을 먹으러 가려고 어디로 갈지 이야기하기 시작한다.
Sarah and Natalie agree to go for lunch and start to talk about where to go.

" 나는 꽤 배고파 " 나탈리가 말한다. " 이탈리아 음식 먹을래? 피자나 파스타 같은 거? "
"I'm rather hungry," says Sarah. "Would you like some Italian food? A pizza or some pasta perhaps?"

나탈리는 결정하지 못한다. " 이탈리아 음식은 좀 별론데. 어디 가서 중국 음식 먹는 건 어때? 괜찮아? "
Natalie is not sure. "I'm not sure I want Italian food. How about a Chinese meal somewhere? Would that be OK?"

사라는 실망하며 햄버거와 감자튀김으로 타협하려 한다. " 대신 햄버거는 어때? " 그녀가 묻는다.
Sarah is disappointed and suggests a burger and chips as a compromise. "Would you like to have a burger instead?" she asks.

" 음… 잘 모르겠는데, " 나탈리가 대답한다. " 감자튀김은 괜찮은데 햄버거는 별로야. "
"Mmmm. I'm not sure I do," answers Natalie. "I like the idea of chips but not the burger."

둘 다 한동안 조용히 생각한다.
They both think silently for a while.

" 그럼 피쉬앤칩스는 어때? " 사라가 묻는다.
"What about fish and chips then?" asks Sarah?

" 그래! " 나탈리가 대답한다. " 딱 좋아! "
"Yes!" says Natalie. "Perfect!"

그들은 피쉬앤칩스 가게로 가서 점심을 주문한다. 둘 다 추가 소금과 식초, 마요네즈를 주문하고 같이 먹을 빵과 버터도 주문한다. 얼마나 완벽한 점심인가!
They go to the fish and chip bar and order their lunch. They both ask for extra salt and vinegar, and mayonnaise, as well as bread and butter to go with it. What a perfect lunch!

피쉬앤칩스와 함께 차를 마시며 쇼핑에 관해 이야기한다.
They drink tea with their fish and chips and chat about their shopping.

사라는 맞는 정장을 찾을 수 없어서 속상하다고 말한다. 나탈리는 매장으로 돌아가서 점원이 추천해 준 정장을 입어보자고 하지만 사라는 다른 곳을 둘러보고 싶다고 한다.
Sarah says she's disappointed not to have found the right suit. Natalie suggests she go back to the department store to try on the suit the shop assistant suggested but Sarah says she wants to look somewhere else.

그들은 점심 후에 다른 가게에 가는 것에 동의한다.
They agree to go to a different shop after lunch.

그들이 함께 들어가자마자, 사라는 그녀가 좋아하는 회색 정장을 본다. 그녀는 입어볼 수 있는지 물어본다.
They walk in together and, immediately, Sarah sees a grey suit that she likes. She asks to try it on.

점원이 사라의 사이즈에 맞는 정장을 찾아 사라가 입어 본다. 그녀가 탈의실 밖으로 나오고 나탈리가 "우와!" 하고는, "딱 맞으면서도 잘 어울려!"라고 말한다.
The shop assistant finds the suit in Sarah's size and Sarah tries it on. She walks out of the changing room and Natalie says, "Wow!", followed by, "That fits you perfectly and looks fantastic!".

사라는 안심하고 미소짓는다. 그녀는 사기로 하고 돈을 내기 위해 지갑에서 신용카드를 꺼낸다. 그녀는 점원에게, "얼마예요?" 하고 묻는다. 그녀는 깜짝 놀랐지만, 정장이 할인판매 중이라 단 150유로라는 것을 알고는 기뻐한다.
Sarah is so relieved and smiles. She decides to buy it and takes her credit card from her purse to pay. She asks the assistant, "How much is that?". She is surprised and pleased to learn the suit is in the sale and only costs €150.

정말 싸게 샀다!
What a bargain!

Difficult Words

1- 파스타 – Pasta
2- 생선 – Fish
3- 추가 – Extra
4- 식초 – Vinegar
5- 가게 점원 – Shop assistant
6- 다른 어딘가 – Somewhere else
7- 곧 – Immediately
8- 탈의실 – Changing room
9- 안도한 – Relieved
10- 지갑 – Purse
11- 기쁜 – Pleased
12- 신용카드 – Credit card
13- 회색 – Grey
14- 정장 – A suit
15- 얼마 – How much

이야기 요약 :

사라와 나탈리는 쇼핑을 계속하지만 우선 점심을 먹기로 한다. 사라는 필요한 모든 것을 찾을 수 있을까 ?

Summary of the Story :

Sarah and Nathalie continue their shopping day, but stop first to eat their lunch. Will Sarah find everything she needs?

이야기 23: 쇼핑과 점심 나들이(2)

Quiz:

1) 옷 가격을 알게 되었을 때 사라의 반응은 ?
   a) 그녀가 생각한 것 보다 비싸서 실망하였다.
   b) 그녀가 생각한 것 보다 저렴해 놀랍고 기뻤다.
   c) 그녀는 가격을 신경 쓰지 않았기 때문에 아무런 반응도 없었다.

1) What is Sarah's reaction when learning the price of the suit?
   a) She is disappointed, because it is more expensive than she thought.
   b) She is surprised and pleased because it is cheaper than she thought.
   c) She doesn't have a reaction, because she doesn't care about the price.

2) 나탈리가 중화요리를 먹기를 권했을때 사라의 반응은 ?
   a) 동의하였다.
   b) 실망하여 따로 먹기를 제안하였다.
   c) 대신 햄버거와 감자튀김 먹기를 제안하였다.

2) What does Sarah do when Nathalie offers her to eat Chinese?
   a) She accepts her idea.
   b) She is disappointed and suggests eating alone.
   c) She suggests eating a hamburger and fries instead.

3) 사라가 자신이 찾는 정장이 없어 실망스럽다고 했을때 나탈리는 무엇을 권하였는가 ?
   a) 다른 가게로 가 계속 돌아보기를 권함
   b) 이전 가게로 돌아가 점원이 추천한 정장을 입어보기를 권유함
   c) 나중에 더 할인이 될 수도 있기 때문에 다른날 다시 오기를 제안함

3) What does Nathalie offer when Sarah tells her that she is disappointed not to have found a suit?
   a) She suggests changing store and keep looking.
   b) She suggests going back to the previous store to try on the suit the shop assistant suggested.
   c) She suggests continuing to look another day when there will have more discount choices.

ANSWERS:
   1) B
   2) C
   3) B

이야기 24: 쇼핑과 점심 나들이(3)
STORY 24: OUT SHOPPING AND FOR LUNCH (3)

사라는 이제 쇼핑하러 나온 것이 좋고 셔츠와 원하는 신발에 대해서 생각하기 시작한다.

Sarah is feeling good about her shopping trip now and starts to think about her shirt and the shoes she wants.

사라와 나탈리는 여성복 셔츠를 보러 백화점 매장으로 돌아가 많은 매장에 다양한 종류가 있다는 것을 알게 된다.

Sarah and Natalie go back to the department store to look for ladies' shirts and find there is a huge choice in a number of departments.

사라는 얼마나 많은 종류 중에서 고를 수 있는지를 보고 감탄하며 그녀의 회색 정장과 함께 입을 셔츠 두 개를 사려고 마음먹었다.

Sarah is amazed how many there are to choose from and decides she will buy two shirts to go with her grey suit.

첫 번째로, 흰 셔츠를 찾는다. 단순하면서도 클래식하다. 그녀는 세 개를 찾아 모두 입어 본다. 하나는 너무 크고, 하나는 너무 작고, 하나는 잘 맞지만, 소매가 너무 길다. 그녀는 계속 찾기로 한다.

First, she looks for a white shirt. Simple and classic. She finds three and tries them on. One is too big, one is too small, and one fits well except the sleeves are too long. She continues looking.

두 개를 더 찾지만 둘 중 하나는 맞는 사이즈를 찾지 못한다. 그녀는 가게 점원에게 그녀의 사이즈가 있는지 묻고 점원은 찾으러 간다. 그녀는 기뻐하며 돌아오고 사라는 셔츠 두 개를 입어본다.

She finds two more but can't find her size in one of them. She asks the shop assistant if they have her size and she goes away to find it. She comes back happy, and Sarah tries on the two shirts.

이번에는, 둘 다 나무랄 데 없어 어려운 결정을 해야만 한다. 이런! 사라는 두 셔츠를 모두 나탈리에게 보여주고 나탈리는 즉시 어느 것을 사야 할지 말해준다.

This time, they are both perfect and she has a difficult decision to make. Oh dear! Sarah shows both shirts to Natalie and, straightaway; Natalie tells her which one to buy.

사라도 동의하고 다른 색깔의 셔츠를 찾기 시작한다. 그녀는 분홍색의 같은 셔츠를 발견하고 기뻐한다. 그래서 사라는 하나는 흰색, 하나는 분홍색의 같은 스타일 셔츠를 두 개 산다.

Sarah agrees and then looks for another shirt in a different colour. She finds the same shirt in pink and she is delighted. So, Sarah buys 2 shirts the same style, one in white and one in pink.

나탈리가 그녀에게 신발도 사야 한다고 다시 한번 알려 주고, 그들은 신발 매장으로 향한다.

Natalie reminds her that they are also looking for shoes, and they head for the shoe department.

사라는 사무용 검은색 신발을 찾기로 하고, 나탈리는 직장에서 신을 남색 신발을 사고 싶다고 한다.

Sarah decides to look for some smart black shoes, and Natalie adds that she wants some navy blue shoes for work.

둘은 바로 남색과 검은색 둘 다 있는 가죽 스마트 신발을 본다. 점원에게 그들의 사이즈를 달라고 하고 - 사라는 사이즈 39이고 나탈리는 37이다 - 놀랍게도, 가게에는 두 사이즈와 두 색이 모두 있다.

They both immediately see some smart leather shoes which seem to be available in both navy blue and black. They ask the assistant for their size – Sarah is a 39 and Natalie is a 37 – and to their surprise, the shop has both sizes in both colours.

그들은 신어 보고, 잠깐 가게를 돌아다닌 후, 사기로 한다.

They try them on, walk around the department for a short while, and then decide to buy them.

사라는 성공적인 쇼핑의 날을 보내고 돈도 많이 쓴 후 집으로 돌아간다. 뭐 할 수 없지...

Sarah goes home having had a very successful shopping day and having spent a great deal of money. Oh well...

Difficult Words

1- 돌아가다 – Go back
2- 매장, 가게 – Departments
3- 놀란 – Amazed
4- 하얀색 – White
5- 소매 – Sleeves
6- 이번 – This time
7- 신 – God
8- 분홍 – Pink
9- 검정색 – Black
10- 네이비색 – Navy
11- 가죽 – Leather
12- 성공적인 – Successful
13- 돈 – Money
14- 이 후에 – After
15- 날, 하루 – A day

이야기 요약 :

사라는 그녀가 필요로한 물건들을 하나 둘씩 찾기 시작하자 점점 쇼핑데이를 즐기게 되었다. 그러나 여전히 그녀는 몇몇 물건들을 더 찾아야 한다.

Summary of the Story :

Sarah is now enjoying her shopping day as she finds more and more items that she is looking for. However, she still has several other things she needs to find.

Quiz:

1) 나탈리는 어떤 색의 신발을 사길 원하였는가?
   a) 검정색
   b) 분홍색
   c) 네이비색

1) What color are the shoes that Nathalie wants to buy?
   a) Black
   b) Pink
   c) Navy blue

2) 사라의 신발 사이즈는 ?
   a) 39
   b) 37
   c) 38

2) What is Sarah's shoes size?
   a) 39
   b) 37
   c) 38

3) 누가 신발을 샀는가?
   a) 사라
   b) 나탈리
   c) 사라와 나탈리

3) Who buys shoes?
   a) Sarah
   b) Nathalie
   c) Sarah et Nathalie

ANSWERS:
   1) C
   2) A
   3) C

이야기 25: 휴가의 마지막 (1)
STORY 25: END OF THE HOLIDAYS (1)

이제 휴가의 마지막 주라 피터는 헨리에게 하고 싶은 것이 있는지 묻는다.

It is the last week of the holidays and Peter asks Henry what he would like to do.

매주, 헨리는 동네 스포츠 센터에 있는 여름 캠프에 가며 친구들을 거기에서 만나기 때문에 평소대로 거기에 가고 싶다고 말한다.

Every week, Henry goes to the summer camp in the local sports centre and he says he still wants to do that as usual as he meets his friends there.

피터는 그 말에 기뻐하며 동의한다. 그러고는 다른 날을 위해 제안을 한다.

Peter is pleased about that and agrees. Then he makes some suggestions for the other days.

"음, 언제 네 새 학교 교복도 사야 하는데." 피터가 말한다.

"Well, we need to buy you some new school uniform one day, I know that." says Peter.

헨리가, "우리 언제 제빵도 하면 안 돼요, 아빠? 우리 제빵 안 한 지 너무 오래됐잖아요." 묻는다.

Henry asks, "Can we do some baking one day, Dad? We haven't done baking for ages."

"네 말이 맞다, 안 한 지 오래됐지," 피터가 동의한다. "우리 초콜릿 케이크나 아니면 스콘을 좀 만들까? 하지만 집안일도 또 해야 하고 집과 정원도 깨끗하게 해야 해."

"You're right, we haven't," agrees Peter. "We could make a chocolate cake and perhaps some scones? But we need to do some housework again and leave the house, and garden, neat and tidy."

헨리는 그가 이번에도 도우리라는 것을 알고 일이 끝나고 나면 보상도 받기를 바란다. 하지만 매주 용돈을 받기 때문에 보상이 없을 수도 있다는 것 또한 잘 알고 있다.

Henry knows he will help with this and hopes he will get a treat at the end. But he also knows he may not because he has pocket money every week.

"찰리 산책 시키는 것부터 시작하자, 어때?" 피터가 헨리에게 제안한다.

"Let's start by taking Charlie for a walk, shall we?" Peter suggests to Henry.

이야기 25: 휴가의 마지막 (1)

"그럼 공원에 갈 수 있어요, 아빠?" 헨리가 묻는다. 헨리는 공원에 공을 가져가 던지면 찰리가 뛰어가 물어 오는 것을 좋아한다.
"Can we go to the park then, Dad?" asks Henry. Henry loves taking a ball to the park and throwing it for Charlie to run after and bring back.

헨리는 위층으로 올라가 산책과 공원에서 놀 때 신을 운동화를 가지러 가고 피터는 찰리의 목줄을 챙긴다. 찰리는 곧바로 산책하러 간다는 것을 알고 흥분한다.
Henry goes upstairs to get his trainers to wear for the walk and to play in the park, and Peter picks up Charlie's lead. Charlie knows straightaway that they're going for a walk and is vey excited.

집 밖으로 나가면서, 그들은 테니스공을 하나 챙긴다.
On the way out of the house, they pick up a tennis ball.

공원까지는 15분이 걸린다. 거기에 도착할 때, 그들이 공원에 있는 유일한 사람이라서 뛰어다니며 놀 수 있는 장소가 많다는 것을 알아차린다. 헨리와 찰리 모두 아주 많이 들떠서 한 시간이 넘도록 행복해하며 뛰어놀고, 던지고, 따라가고, 잡기와 가져오기를 한다.
It takes fifteen minutes to get to the park. When they get there, they find they are the only people in the park so they have lots of space to run around and play. Henry and Charlie are both very excited and play happily for more than an hour, throwing, chasing, catching and fetching.

둘은 모두 지쳐서 헨리는 그네에 앉고 찰리는 근처 바닥에 눕는다. 그들은 돌아가기 전에 몇 분 동안 쉰다.
They are both exhausted so Henry sits on a swing and Charlie lies on the ground nearby. They wait a few minutes before they walk back.

집으로 돌아오는 길에, 헨리는, "아빠, 내 운동화가 이제 너무 작은 것 같아요. 우리 내일 새 교복도 사고 운동화도 사러 갈 수 있어요?" 말한다.
As they are walking home, Henry says, "Dad, I think my trainers are too small now. Can we go shopping for my new school uniform tomorrow and buy some trainers as well?"

"그래, 그러자. 좋은 생각이야," 피터가 말한다.
"Yes, we can. Good idea," says Peter.

Difficult Words

1- 주 – Week
2- 여름 – Summer
3- 평소대로 – As usual
4- 친구들 – Friends
5- 정원 – Garden
6- 정돈된 – Tidy
7- 바라다 – Hope
8- 용돈 – Pocket money
9- 던지기 – Throwing
10- 운동화 – Trainers
11- 개 목줄 – Lead
12- 쫓기 – Chasing
13- 잡기 – Catching
14- 그네 – Swing
15- 지친 – Exhausted

이야기 요약 :

방학의 마지막 주를 맞아 피터와 헨리는 찰리를 데리고 공원에 가서 휴일의 남은 날 동안 무엇을 할지 계획한다.

Summary of the Story :

It's the last week of vacation and Peter and Henry take the opportunity to go to the park with their dog Charlie and plan what they will do during their last days of rest.

Quiz:

1) 공원에서 돌아와 해야 할 집안일들은?
   a) 스콘과 초콜렛 케이크 만들기
   b) 집과 정원 청소하기
   c) 청소기를 밀고 식료품점 가기

1) What are the choirs they need to do after their walk in the park?
   a) To cook scones and chocolate cake.
   b) To clean the house and the garden.
   c) To vacuum and do the grocery.

2) 그들은 얼마나 공원에 머물것인가?
   a) 15분
   b) 한 시간 이상
   c) 아침 내내

2) How long do they stay in the park?
   a) 15 minutes
   b) More than an hour
   c) All morning

3) 공원에는 :
   a) 아무도 없었다
   b) 사람이 거의 없어서 뛰어놀 공간이 많았다
   c) 많은 사람들이 있었다

3) In the park, there is:
   a) Nobody else
   b) Few people, but lots of space to run around and play
   c) Lots of people

ANSWERS:
   1) B
   2) B
   3) A

이야기 26: 휴가의 마지막 (2)
STORY 26: END OF THE HOLIDAYS (2)

이번 주가 휴가의 마지막 주다. 피터와 헨리는 할 일 목록이 있다.

It is the last week of the holidays. Peter and Henry have a list of things to do.

오늘은 새 학교 교복과 특히, 새 운동화를 사기로 한 날이다.

Today is the day for buying new school uniform and, in particular, new trainers.

피터는 학교 교복 목록을 찾아 헨리와 함께 살펴보기 시작한다. 피터가 항목을 말하면, 헨리가 작년 교복을 찾아 여전히 맞는지 입어본다. 맞지 않으면, 쇼핑 리스트에 적는다. 맞으면 다행히, 살 것이 하나 줄어든다.

Peter finds the school uniform list and starts to go through it with Henry. Peter says the item, and Henry finds the uniform from last year and tries it on to see if it still fits. If it doesn't, it goes on the shopping list. If it does, good, one less thing to buy.

피터가, "목록 제일 위쪽에 새 운동화를 넣자. 작아서 못 신으니까." 라고 말한다. 그리고 그들은 목록 작성을 시작한다.

Peter says, "Let's put new trainers at the top of the list. We know they're too small." And they start the list.

쇼핑 목록:

SHOPPING LIST:

- 운동화
- Trainers

헨리는 반바지와 긴바지를 입어보고 반바지는 맞지만, 긴바지는 이제 너무 짧다는 것을 알아차린다.

Henry tries on his shorts and trousers and finds the shorts fit, but the trousers are too short now.

- 운동화
- 진회색 긴 바지 두 개
- Trainers
- 2 pairs of dark grey trousers

이제 폴로셔츠를 입어본다. 이것들도 이제 너무 짧고, 하얗다기보다는 회색에 가까워서 피터는 그것도 목록에 넣기로 한다.

Then they try on the polo shirts. They are also too short now, and they look grey rather than white, so Peter adds those to the list as well.

- 운동화
- 진회색 긴 바지 두 개
- 흰색 폴로 셔츠 5개
- Trainers
- 2 pairs of dark grey trousers
- 5 white polo shirts

" 운동복 상의는 어디에 있니, 헨리야? " 피터가 묻는다.
"Where is your sweatshirt, Henry?" asks Peter.

" 끝까지 못 찾았어요, 아빠. 확실히 새것이 필요해요. "
"I couldn't find it at the end of term, Dad. I definitely need a new one."

- 운동화
- 진회색 긴 바지 두 개
- 흰색 폴로 셔츠 5개
- 빨간 운동복 상의
- Trainers
- 2 pairs of dark grey trousers
- 5 white polo shirts
- Red sweatshirt

" 운동화랑 같이, 체육복은 어때? 체육 수업에 필요한 새 반바지 필요하니? " 피터가 헨리에게 묻는다.
"As well as trainers, what about your PE kit? Do you need any new shorts for PE?" Peter asks Henry.

" 입어볼게요, " 헨리가 대답한다. 바지는 아직 맞지만, 체육 시간에 신을 새 양말이 필요하다.
"I'll try them on," replies Henry. He finds that they still fit, but he needs new PE socks.

- 운동화
- 진회색 긴 바지 두 개
- 흰색 폴로 셔츠 5개
- 빨간 운동복 상의
- 체육용 흰 양말
- Trainers
- 2 pairs of dark grey trousers

- 5 white polo shirts
- Red sweatshirt
- White PE socks

"내 생각에 새 회색 양말도 필요할 것 같은데, 헨리, 그것들도 목록에 넣자," 피터가 제안한다.

"I think you need new grey socks as well, Henry, so let's put those on the list as well," Peter suggests.

- 운동화
- 진회색 긴 바지 두 개
- 흰색 폴로 셔츠 5개
- 빨간 운동복 상의
- 체육용 흰 양말
- 회색 양말 5켤레
- Trainers
- 2 pairs of dark grey trousers
- 5 white polo shirts
- Red sweatshirt
- White PE socks
- 5 pairs of grey socks

마지막으로, 헨리의 등교 신발에 대해 생각해본다. 헨리가 신어 보더니, 운동화와 마찬가지로 이제 너무 작아져서 그것도 쇼핑 목록에 들어가야 한다.

And finally, they think about Henry's school shoes. Henry tries them on and, like his trainers, they are now too small, so they also need to go on the shopping list.

피터가 제안한다.

Peter suggests.

- 운동화
- 진회색 긴 바지 두 개
- 흰색 폴로 셔츠 5개
- 빨간 운동복 상의
- 체육용 흰 양말
- 회색 양말 5켤레
- 검은색 등교 신발
- Trainers

- 2 pairs of dark grey trousers
- 5 white polo shirts
- Red sweatshirt
- White PE socks
- 5 pairs of grey socks
- Black school shoes

피터와 헨리 둘 다 목록을 보고 바쁜 쇼핑이 기다리고 있음을 예감한다.

*참고: PE = Physical Education으로, 체육수업을 말한다.

Peter and Henry both look at the list and agree they have a busy day of shopping ahead of them.

Difficullt Words

이야기 요약 :

오늘 피터와 헨리는 쇼핑데이 계획을 세우고, 헨리가 학교에 돌아가기 위해 필요한 모든 것들의 목록을 정리하고 있다.

Summary of the Story :

Today Peter and Henry are planning their shopping day and making a list of everything they need for Henry's return to school.

Quiz:

1) 몇 개의 하얀색 폴로 셔츠가 필요한가?

   a) 2

   b) 5

   c) 1

1) How many white polo shirts do they need?

   a) 2

   b) 5

   c) 1

2) 운동복의 색은 ?

   a) 하얀색

   b) 검정색

   c) 붉은색

2) What color is the sweatshirt?

   a) White

   b) Black

   c) Red

3) 전부 몇 켤레의 양말을 사야 하는가 ?

   a) 20

   b) 10

   c) 5

3) In total, how many socks do they need to buy?

   a) 20

   b) 10

   c) 5

ANSWERS:

   1) B

   2) C

   3) B

이야기 27: 휴가의 마지막 (3)
STORY 27: END OF THE HOLIDAYS (3)

학교 교복 쇼핑 목록을 손에 들고, 피터와 헨리는 시내로 운전하러 나가기 위해 차를 탄다.

With the school uniform shopping list in hand, Peter and Henry get into the car to drive to town.

도착해서는 운동화를 사러 스포츠용품점을 먼저 들린다. 헨리는 4개의 다른 운동화를 신어본다 - 모두 흰색 운동화 한 켤레, 파란색과 흰색이 섞인 것 한 켤레, 빨간색과 검은색이 섞인 것 한 켤레, 마지막으로 흰색과 초록색이 섞인 것 한 켤레. 피터는 파란색과 흰색이 섞인 것이 제일 괜찮아 보인다고 생각했지만, 헨리는 그가 제일 좋아하는 축구팀을 떠올리게 한다며 빨간색과 검은색이 섞인 것을 원한다. 그게 더 비싸지만, 피터는 빨간색과 검은색 운동화에 찬성한다.

When they arrive, they go first to a sports shop to buy some trainers. Henry tries on 4 different pairs – one all white pair, one pair that is blue and white, one pair that is red and black, and finally a white and green pair. Peter thinks the blue and white look best but Henry wants the red and black, because they remind him of his favourite football team. They cost more, but Peter agrees to the red and black pair.

그들은 스포츠용품점에서 헨리의 체육용 흰 양말을 산다.

While they are in the sports shop, they buy Henry's white PE socks.

그리고는 신발을 포함해 다른 다섯 개의 물건을 사러 유명한 백화점으로 간다.

They then go to a well-known department store to look for the other five items, including the shoes.

그들은 즉시 흰 폴로셔츠를 발견하고 헨리가 필요한 셔츠 다섯 개를 쇼핑 바구니에 넣는다. 폴로셔츠 근처에 여러 색상의 운동복 상의도 있다: 남색, 초록색, 보라색, 노란색 그리고 다행히, 빨간색. 그래서, 헨리의 사이즈에 맞는 빨간 운동복 상의도 쇼핑 바구니에 넣는다.

They find the white polo shirts straightaway and are able to put the five shirts Henry needs into the shopping basket. Near to the polo shirts are the sweatshirts in different colours: navy blue, green, purple, yellow and, thankfully, red. So, a red sweatshirt in Henry's size goes into the shopping basket.

회색 양말도 찾기 쉽다 - 맞는 사이즈도 많다. 다섯 켤레를 쇼핑 바구니에 넣는다.

The grey socks are just as easy to find – there are plenty in the right size. Five pairs go into the shopping basket.

고를 수 있는 긴바지도 많다 - 적어도 피터는 그렇게 생각한다. 그는 선반에 있는 거의 모든 바지를 보지만 헨리에게 맞는 사이즈는 딱 하나만 있다. 피터는 그것을 바구니에 넣고 점원을 찾으려고 한다. 하지만 헨리가 학교에 개학 후 첫 몇 주 동안은 반바지를 입을 것이기 때문에 온라인으로 주문하고 도착할 때까지 기다릴 수 있어서 걱정하지 않기로 한다.

There are plenty of trousers to choose from as well – or so Peter thinks. He looks at nearly every pair on the racks and only finds one pair that are the right size for Henry. Peter puts them in the basket and tries to find an assistant. But then Peter decides not to worry as Henry will wear shorts for the first few weeks back at school, and they can order a pair online and wait for them to arrive.

그들은 계산대로 가서 바구니에 담긴 물건들을 계산한다.

They go to the till and pay for the items in the basket.

이제 신발이다. 그들은 고를 수 있는 선택이 많은 신발 매장으로 간다. 끈이 달린 것도 있고 찍찍이가 달린 것도 있다. 피터는 끈이 달린 신발이 더 낫다고 판단하고, 헨리는 편하다고 한 신발 한 켤레를 신어본다. 지적으로 보이기도 한다. 그래서, 피터가 신발도 계산한다.

And now the shoes. They go to the shoe department where there are many pairs to choose from. Some with laces, some with Velcro straps. Peter decides that laced shoes are better and Henry tries on a pair that he says are really comfortable. They look smart as well. So, Peter pays for the shoes as well.

들어야 할 짐이 많아서, 피터는 집에 돌아가기 전에 뭔가 마시자고 제안한다. 헨리는 쇼핑 때문에 배가 고프다며 뭔가 먹어도 되냐고 물어본다.

With lots of bags to carry, Peter suggests they go for a drink before going home. Henry asks if he can have something to eat as shopping makes him hungry.

피터는 커피와 케이크를, 헨리는 코카콜라와 케이크를 먹는다.

Coffee and cake for Peter, Coca-Cola and cake for Henry.

Difficult Words

1- 스포츠 용품 매장 – Sports shop
2- 유명한 – Well known
3- 포함한 – Including
4- 바구니 – Basket
5- 보라색 – Purple
6- 노란색 – Yellow
7- 선반 – Racks
8- 걱정하다 – To worry
9- 입을 것이다 – Will wear
10- 주문하다 – To order
11- 신반 끈 – Laces
12- 찍찍이 – Velcro straps
13- 편안한 – Comfortable
14- (짐을)들다, 나르다 – To carry
15- 제안하다 – Suggests

이야기 요약 :

쇼핑 목록이 마무리 되어 피터와 헨리는 필요한 모든 것을 구매하기 위해 쇼핑센터로 향한다. 과연 하루 안에 필요한 모든 것을 찾을 수 있을 것인가?

Summary of the Story :

Now that their shopping list is complete, Peter and Henry go to the shopping center to buy everything they need. Will they manage to find everything in one day?

이야기 27: 휴가의 마지막 (3)

Quiz:

1) 제일 처음 구매한 물품은?
   a) 운동화
   b) 양말
   c) 바지

1) What is the first item that they buy?
   a) Trainers
   b) Socks
   c) Trousers

2) 피터와 헨리가 선택한 신발은 어떤 것인가?
   a) 신발끈이 달린 신발
   b) 찍찍이가 달린 신말
   c) 신발끈과 찍찍이가 달린 신발

2) How are the shoes that Peter and Henry choose?
   a) With laces
   b) With Velcro straps
   c) With laces and Velcro straps

3) 헨리는 무엇을 사먹었나?
   a) 커피와 케이크
   b) 코카콜라와 케이크
   c) 레모네이드와 쿠키

3) What does Henry buy to eat?
   a) A coffee and a cake
   b) A Coca Cola and a cake
   c) Lemonade and a cookie

ANSWERS:
   1) A
   2) A
   3) B

LECTURA 28 : 휴가의 마지막 (4)
STORY 28: END OF THE HOLIDAYS (4)

오늘은 동네 스포츠 센터에서 하는 헨리의 마지막 여름 캠프 날이다.
Today is Henry's last day at the Summer Camp in the local sports centre.

그는 일어나서 수영복과 수건을 가방에 챙기고, 새 운동화를 꺼낸다.
When he gets up, he packs his bag with his swimming costume and towel, and gets out his new trainers.

는 축구복을 입고 새 운동화를 신은 후 아침을 먹으러 아래층으로 내려간다. 피터는 벌써 아래층에서 헨리의 점심 샌드위치를 만들고 있고, 오늘 헨리가 여름 캠프에서 무엇을 할지에 대해 이야기한다.
Peter is downstairs already making Henry's sandwich for lunch, and they talk about what Henry might do today at the summer camp.

" 글쎄요, 우리는 항상 축구 경기를 해요. 그게 제일 신나는 부분이에요. 여섯 팀과 교체선수를 몇 명 할 만큼 사람 수도 충분하고 하루 동안 토너먼트로 경기해요. 경기 중간에, 수영을 갈 수도 있고, 배드민턴을 할 수도 있어요, " 헨리가 설명한다.
"Well, we always play football. That's the best part. There are enough people for six teams and a few substitutes, and we play a tournament during the day. In between games, we can go swimming, or play badminton," Henry explains.

" 다른 것도 할 게 많아요, " 헨리가 덧붙인다.
"There are other things to do as well, we choose," Henry adds.

사려 깊게, 그는, " 오늘은 다른 액티비티도 해보려고요, 캠프에서의 마지막 날인 만큼. " 이라고 한다.
Thoughtfully, he says, "I think that I will try some different activities today as well, as it is my last day at camp."

" 양궁이 재밌을 것 같아요, " 헨리가 말한다. " 어떻게 생각하세요, 아빠? "
"I like the idea of archery," Henry says. "What do you think, Dad?"

" 좋은 생각이야. 해봐. 재밌을 것 같은데. 다른 액티비티는 어떤 게 있니? " 피터가 묻는다.
"Great. Have a go. It sounds like fun. And what other activities are there to do?" Peter asks.

LECTURA 28 : 휴가의 마지막 (4)

리가 대답하기를, "글쎄요, 수영장에서 카누도 탈 수 있어요. 하고 싶지는 않지만요. 트램펄린도 있고요, 농구도 있는 것 같아요."
Henry replies, "Well, there's canoeing in the swimming pool. I don't think I want to do that though. There's also trampolining, and basketball, I think."

"하고 싶으면 모든 액티비티를 다 할 수 있니?" 피터가 헨리에게 묻는다.
"Can you do all of the activities if you want to?" Peter asks Henry.

"네," 헨리가 대답하며, "축구 경기 중간에 해야 하지만요!"
"Yes," Henry answers, "You just have to do them between the football matches!"

그들은 헨리의 점심을 배낭에 넣는다. 헨리가 아침을 다 먹은 후 그들은 집을 나선다.
They put Henry's packed lunch into his rucksack. Henry finishes his breakfast, and they leave.

찰리가 혼자 남을 하루 생각에 슬퍼 보인다.
Charlie looks sad at the thought of a day on his own.

피터는 스포츠 센터로 운전해 주차하고, 헨리를 등록 창구로 데려간다. 많은 직원과 헨리처럼 활력이 넘치는 아이들 또한 많이 있다. 그들은 서로 만나 행복하고 들떠 보이고 피터는 헨리가 신나는 하루를 보내리라는 것을 안다.
Peter drives to the sports centre, parks, and takes Henry up to the registration desk. There are lots of staff there, as well as lots of energetic children, just like Henry. They look happy and excited to see each other and Peter knows that Henry is going to have a great day.

그리고 피터도!
And so is Peter!

Difficult Words

1- 마지막 – Last
2- 수영복 – Swimming costume
3- 수건 – Towel
4- 가방에 넣다 – Packs
5- 최고 – Best
6- 팀 – Teams
7- 교체선수 – Substitutes
8- 우리는 선택한다 – We choose
9- 토너먼트 – A tournament
10- 양궁 – Archery
11- 카누 – Canoeing
12- 접수대 – Registration desk
13- 어린이들 – Children
14- 트램펄린 – Trampolining
15- 배낭 – Rucksack

이야기 요약 :

오늘은 헨리가 다니는 지역 스포츠 센터의 여름 캠프 마지막 날이다. 이 날은 친구들도 만나고 새로운 활동도 시도해 볼 수 있는 축구 토너먼트 날이어서 헨리는 무척이나 기쁘다.

Summary of the Story :

Today is Henry's last day at the summer camp in the local sports center. He is very excited because it is the day of the football tournament where he can see his friends and try new activities.

LECTURA 28 : 휴가의 마지막 (4)

Quiz:

1) 헨리가 입은 오늘 입은 옷은?
   a) 체육 반바지와 새 운동화
   b) 하얀 새 폴로 셔츠와 체육 반바지
   c) 축구복과 새 운동화

1) What is Henry's outfit today?
   a) A Sport short with his new trainers.
   b) His new white polo with his sport short.
   c) His football kit and new trainers.

2) 몇명의 팀을 생성할 만큼의 선수들이 있는가?
   a) 5
   b) 6
   c) 7

2) There are enough players to create how many teams?
   a) 5
   b) 6
   c) 7

3) 카누를 할 수 있는 곳은 어디인가?
   a) 축구장 근처 강
   b) 축구장 근처 호수
   c) 수영장

3) Where is located the canoeing activity?
   a) In the river near the football field.
   b) In the lake near the football field.
   c) In the swimming pool.

ANSWERS:
   1) C
   2) B
   3) C

이야기 29: 휴가의 마지막 (5)
STORY 29: END OF THE HOLIDAYS (5)

헨리는 여름 캠프에 있고 오늘이 피터에게는 다음 주에 선생님으로 직장에 복귀하기 전 하고 싶은 것을 다 할 수 있는 휴가의 마지막 날이다.

Henry is at summer camp and today is the last day of the holidays when Peter can do whatever he wants to do before he goes back to work as a teacher next week.

피터는 찰리를 데리고 긴 산책을 하러 나간다. 그들은 공원으로 간 다음 들판을 가로질러 걷고 8km가 넘게 걸은 후 집에 도착한다. 찰리는 잠을 오래 자려고 눕는다.

Peter takes Charlie for a long walk. They go to the park and then walk through the fields and arrive home after eight kilometres. Charlie lies down for a long sleep.

피터는 이른 점심을 준비하기 위해 주방으로 들어가 오후 동안 진짜 하고 싶은 것이 무엇인지 생각해본다.

Peter goes into the kitchen to prepare an early lunch and stops to think about what he really wants to do during the afternoon.

어떤 선택권이 있을까?

What are his options?

집에서 TV를 볼 수 있다. 아니, 그건 언제든 원할 때면 할 수 있다.

He can stay at home and watch TV. No, he can do that whenever he wants to.

다음 주에 먹을 식료품 쇼핑을 하러 갈 수도 있다. 아니, 원할 때면 언제든 온라인으로 식료품을 주문할 수 있다.

He can go shopping to buy food for next week. No, he can shop online for food whenever he wants to.

골프를 한 경기 하러 갈 수도 있다. 아니, 그건 다른 사람과 함께 가는 것이 더 좋고, 혼자 하는 것은 좋아하지 않는다.

He can go and play a round of golf. No, he would rather have company to do that, he doesn't like playing on his own.

수영을 갈 수 있다. 아니, 아직 스포츠 센터로 돌아가기 싫다.

He can go for a swim. No, he doesn't want to go back to the sports centre yet.

그는 잔디를 깎고 집을 청소하고 세차를 하고 화장실 청소를 할 수 있다. 아니, 내일 헨리의 도움을 받아 할 것이다. 그러는 편이 더 재밌다.

He can mow the lawn, clean the house, wash the car, and clean the bathrooms. No, he will do that tomorrow with Henry's help. That will be more fun.

새 직장에서 입을 옷을 쇼핑하러 갈 수 있다.
He can go shopping for some new work clothes.

사실, 나쁜 생각이 아니다.
Actually, that isn't a bad idea.

그러고는 다른 생각이 났다. 그는 사라에게 전화한다.
Then he has another idea. He phones Sarah.

" 아직 점심 안 먹었지? " 그는 그녀가 전화를 받자마자 물어본다.
"Have you had lunch yet?" he asks her as she answers the phone.

" 아직. 점심시간까지 30분 남았어, " 그녀가 대답한다.
"Not yet. I take my lunch in about half an hour," she replies.

" 잘됐다. 그럼 같이 점심 먹자, " 피터가 그녀에게 말한다. " 새 옷 좀 사러 시내에 갈 거거든. 내 휴가도 거의 끝나가는데 우리 둘이서 조용하게 점심 먹으면 되겠다. "
"Fantastic. Let's have lunch together then," Peter says to her. "I'm coming to town to buy some new clothes. We can have a quiet lunch together as my holiday is nearly over."

" 그럼 너무 좋겠다, " 사라가 긍정적으로 대답한다. " 하이(High) 거리 코너에 있는 이탈리아 레스토랑에서 만나. 너무 기대된다! "
"That would be lovely," Sarah replies, positively. "I will meet you at the Italian restaurant on the corner of the High Street. I am really looking forward to it!"

피터는 기뻐하며 옷을 갈아입기 위해 위층으로 뛰어 올라간다.
Peter is very pleased and runs upstairs to get changed.

Difficult Words

1- 들판 – Fields
2- 눕다 – Lies down
3- 자다 – Sleep
4- 오후 – Afternoon
5- 시청하다 – To watch
6- 그가 원할 땐 언제든지 – Whenever he wants to
7- 그가 전화를 하다 – He phones
8- 반 – Half
9- 조용한 – Quiet
10- 위층 – Upstairs
11- 나쁜 – Bad
12- 차 – Car
13- 그는 좋아하지 않는다 – He doesn't like
14- 오늘 – Today
15- 여덟 – Eight

이야기 요약 :

헨리가 여름 캠프에 가 있는 동안, 피터는 그의 마지막 휴일에 무엇을 하기 원하는지 생각해 본다. 다음날 직장으로 복귀해야 하기 때문이다. 결정을 내리기 전 여러 선택사항을 고려해 본다.

Summary of the Story :

While Henry is busy at the summer camp, Peter thinks about what he wants to do on his last day of vacation since he goes back to work the next day. He considers several options before choosing one.

Quiz:

1) 왜 피터는 다음주치 식료품 쇼핑을 하길 원하지 않았는가 ?
   a) 혼자 식료품 쇼핑에 가기 싫어서
   b) 시내로 나가기 싫어서
   c) 온라인으로 언제든지 장을 볼 수 있어서

1) Why doesn't he want to go grocery shopping for next week?
   a) Because he doesn't like to do the grocery alone.
   b) Because he doesn't want to go back in town.
   c) Because he can shop online whenever he wants to.

2) 왜 사라에게 전화를 했는가?
   a) 점심을 이미 먹었는지 물어보기 위해서
   b) 그녀의 상태가 좋아졌는지 묻기 위해서
   c) 그가 무얼 하면 좋을지 그녀의 조언을 얻기 위해서

2) Why is he calling Sarah?
   a) To ask if she had lunch already.
   b) To ask if she feel better.
   c) To ask an advice on what he should do of his day.

3) 사라는 어떤 음식점을 제안했는가 ?
   a) 이태리 음식점
   b) 중국 음식점
   c) 베트남 음식점

3) What restaurant does Sarah offer?
   a) An Italian restaurant
   b) A Chinese restaurant
   c) A Vietnamese restaurant

ANSWERS:
   1) C
   2) A
   3) A

이야기 30: 휴가의 마지막 (6)
STORY 30: END OF THE HOLIDAYS (6)

피터와 헨리는 휴가 마지막 날에 아침 식사를 함께한다. 사라는 일찍 일하러 갔다.

Peter and Henry are having breakfast together on the last day of the holidays. Sarah has gone to work early.

"헨리, 오늘, 우리 집안일을 전부 다 해야 다음 주에 학교로 돌아갈 때 집을 깨끗이 정돈된 상태로 유지할 수 있어," 피터가 말한다.

"Henry, today, we need to do all the household jobs so that we leave the house clean and tidy when we go back to school next week," says Peter.

헨리가 미소를 지으며 말하기를, "알아요, 아빠. 오늘 좀 힘든 일을 해야죠. 그래도 그다음에 빵 만들 수 있을까요?"

Henry smiles and says, "I know, Dad. I know we have to do some hard work today. Can we do some baking afterwards though?"

피터도 해야 할 일을 모두 끝낸 후 오후에 제빵 하는 것에 찬성한다.

Peter agrees to a baking afternoon when they have finished doing all their jobs.

헨리는 또 세차하겠다고 한다 - 그는 전에도 재밌어하며 잘 해냈다.

Henry offers to clean the car again – he enjoyed that and did it well last time.

피터는 그에게 먼저, 침실을 정리·정돈하고, 가방을 싸놓고, 교복을 준비해야 한다고 말한다.

Peter tells him that first, he has to make sure that his bedroom is tidy, his school bag is packed, and his uniform is ready.

헨리는 자기 방을 정리하는 일이 기쁘지 않아서 천천히 위층으로 올라간다.

Henry isn't happy at having to tidy his bedroom, and goes upstairs slowly.

피터는 식기세척기에 접시들을 넣고, 주방을 청소하고, 주방 바닥을 밀 대질한다. 이제, 주방은 거의 끝났다.

Peter puts the dishes in the dishwasher, cleans the kitchen, then mops the kitchen floor. Now, the kitchen is more or less done.

피터는 화장실 청소를 시작하기 위해 위층으로 올라간다. 그는 화장실 청소는 좋아하지 않는다.

Peter then walks upstairs to the bathrooms to start cleaning there. He doesn't like cleaning the bathrooms.

이야기 30: 휴가의 마지막 (6)

그 일이 끝났을 때, 세탁기에 빨아야 할 옷이 있다는 것도 생각난다. 그리고는 침대보를 바꾼다.
When he finishes that, he remembers to put some washing in the washing machine. Then he changes the beds.

피터는 헨리에게 잔디를 깎으러 밖으로 나간다고 말한다. 그가 방에 있는 것을 발견하고는 방이 깨끗해 보이니 이제 세차하러 가면 된다고 말한다.
Peter tells Henry that he's going outside to mow the lawn. He finds him in his bedroom and tells him that his bedroom is looking tidy so he can go and clean the car now.

피터와 헨리는 아래층으로 함께 내려간다. 피터는 잔디를 깎고 헨리는 세차한다.
Peter and Henry go downstairs together. Peter mows the lawn and Henry cleans the car.

또다시, 헨리는 훌륭하게 일을 해내고 일이 끝났을 때 차가 매우 반짝이고 있었다.
Again, Henry does a very good job and the car is very shiny when he finishes.

피터가 끝났을 때 정원 또한 보기 좋았다.
The garden looks good when Peter finishes, as well.

그들은 점심시간임을 알아차리고 정원에 함께 앉아 샌드위치를 먹는다.
They realise it's time for lunch now so they sit down together in the garden and eat a sandwich.

그들은 행복하게 오전에 한 일을 떠올리며 오후에는 제빵을 하기로 동의한다.
They reflect happily on what they have done this morning, and agree that they are going to do some baking in the afternoon.

" 어떤 것부터 만들까? 초콜릿 케이크 아니면 스콘? " 피터가 헨리에게 묻는다.
"Which shall we make first? The chocolate cake or the scones?" Peter asks Henry.

헨리는 잠시 생각한 후, " 엄마가 초콜릿 케이크를 좋아하니 스콘부터 만들어요. 그러면 엄마가 도착했을 때 케이크가 더 따뜻해서 엄마가 좋아할 거예요! " 라고 말한다.
Henry thinks for a moment and says, "Mum loves chocolate cake so let's make the scones first. The cake will be warmer when Mum gets home and she will love it!".

Difficult Words

1- 일찍 – Early
2- 열심히 – Hard
3- 접시 – Dishes
4- 바닥 – The floor
5- 대략 – More or less
6- 끝마친 – Done
7- 세탁기 – Washing machine
8- 사랑하다 – To love
9- 더 따뜻하다 – Warmer
10- 빛나는 – Shiny
11- 아래층으로 내려가다 – Go downstairs
12- 전에 – Last time
13- 화장실 – Bathrooms
14- 행복하게 – Happily
15- 좋아 보이다 – Looks good

이야기 요약 :

휴가의 마지막 날이 되었고 피터와 헨리는 각각 학교와 직장으로 돌아가기 전 많은 일을 해야 한다. 둘은 누가 무슨 일을 하고 보상으로 어떤 활동을 할 것인지를 정했다.

Summary of the Story :

It's the last day of vacation and Peter and Henry have a lot of work to do before going back to school and work. They decide together who will do what and what activity they will do as a reward.

Quiz:

1) 헨리가 가장 먼저 해야 하는 일은 ?
   a) 세차하기
   b) 화장실 청소하기
   c) 자기방 청소하기

1) What is the first task that Henry have to do?
   a) Clean the car
   b) Clean the bathroom
   c) Clean his room

2) 헨리는 방학 마지막 날에 집안일을 해야한다는 아이디어에 어떻게 반응 하였는가 ?
   a) 행복해 하지 않았다.
   b) 미소지으며 열심히 일할 준비가 되 있었다.
   c) 집안일에 기여할지 말지 선택권이 없었기 때문에 아무것도 느끼지 않았다.

2) How does Henry react at the idea of having to do housework on their last day of vacation?
   a) He is not happy.
   b) He smiles and is ready to work hard.
   c) He has no emotion because he has no choice to contribute in the housework chore.

3) 다음 중 피터가 하지 않은 일은?
   a) 부엌 청소하기
   b) 세차하기
   c) 침대보 갈기

3) Which of the following task Peter does not do?
   a) Clean the kitchen
   b) Clean the car
   c) Change the sheets

ANSWERS:
   1) C
   2) B
   3) B

CONCLUSION

You have just completed the 30 short stories in this book. Congratulations!

We hope that the collection of stories you have read will encourage you to continue learning Korean. Reading can be one of the best---and most enjoyable--activities you could do to develop your language skills. Hopefully, you were able to experience that with this book.

If fully consumed as we have intended, these Korean short stories would widen your Korean vocabulary and the audio would allow you to follow along to the words, expose you to correct Korean pronunciation, and help you practice your listening comprehension.

If you need more help with learning Korean, please visit www.fluentinkorean.com.

Cheers and best of luck to you!

Fluent in Korean Team

HOW TO DOWNLOAD THE AUDIO?

INSTRUCTIONS ON HOW TO DOWNLOAD THE AUDIO

Please take note that the audio are in MP3 format and need to be accessed online. No worries though; it's quite easy! Simply follow the instructions below. It will teach you the steps on where and how to download this book's accompanying audio.

On your computer, smartphone, iphone/ipad or tablet, go to this link:

http://fluentinkorean.com/mp3-korean-stories/

Do you have any problems downloading the audio? If you do, feel free to send an email to contact@fluentinkorean.com. We'll do our best to assist you, but we would greatly appreciate if you thoroughly review the instructions first.

Thank you.

ABOUT FLUENT IN KOREAN

Fluentinkorean.com believes that Korean can be learned almost painlessly with the help of a learning habit. Through its website and the books and audiobooks that it offers, Korean language learners are treated to high quality materials that are designed to keep them motivated until they reach their language learning goals.

Keep learning Korean and enjoy the learning process with books and audio from Fluent in Korean.

Printed in Great Britain
by Amazon